THE FIRST EUROPEANS

**The early peoples of Europe
and the rise of Greece and Rome**

Devised and produced by Andrea Dué
Text by Renzo Rossi

MACMILLAN LIBRARY REFERENCE USA
NEW YORK

INTRODUCTION

First published in Italian by Jaca Book
© Editoriale Jaca Book Spa, Milano
1993

This edition published 1996
by Macmillan Library Reference USA
866 Third Avenue
New York, NY 10022

English Language Translation
Copyright © Simon and Schuster
Macmillan 1996

Text by Renzo Rossi, Cinzia Bearzot
Scientific adviser Cinzia Bearzot
Edited by Brian Williams,
Martina Veutro
Translation by Patricia Borlenghi
Art director Roberto Simoni
Colour illustrations by Simone Boni,
Giuseppe Cicio, Francesca D'Ottavi,
Cecco Mariniello, Paolo Ravaglia,
Lorenzo Pieri, designed by Lorenzo
Pieri, Paolo Ravaglia, Roberto Simoni
Maps plans and models by Alessandro
Bartolozzi, Roberto Simoni, Chiara
Pignaris
Black and white illustrations by
Alessandro Baldanzi, Alessandro
Bosher, Lorenzo Cecchi, Asli Falaj,
Paolo Ravaglia, Lorenzo Pieri, Roberto
Simoni

Produced by AS Publishing
Library of Congress Cataloging-in-
Publication Data

Rossi, Renzo, 1940-
[Atlanti della storia dell'uomo.
English]
The atlas of human history/devised
and produced by Andrea Dué; text by
Renzo Rossi.
p.; cm.
Includes indexes.
Contents: [1] The first people – [2]
The first settlers – [3] Cradles of
civilization – [4] The first Europeans –
[5] Civilizations of Asia – [6]
Civilizations of the Americas.
ISBN 0-02-860285-4 (v. 1). –
ISBN 0-02-860286-2 (v. 2). –
ISBN 0-02-860287-0 (v. 3). –
ISBN 0-02-860288-9 (v. 4) –
ISBN 0-02-860289-7 (v. 5). –
ISBN 0-02-860290-0 (v. 6)
1. History, Ancient – Maps for
children. 2. Historical geography –
Maps for children. 3. Children's atlases.
[1. Civilization, Ancient – Maps.
2. Historical geography – Maps.
3. Atlases.]
I. Dué, Andrea. II. Title.
G1033.R6 1996 <G&M>
930–dc20   95-8622
                              CIP
                           MAP AC

Printed and bound in Italy by Grafiche
Editoriali Padane Spa, Cremona

The first European civilizations developed during the Bronze and Iron Ages, from about 3000 to 500 BC. This period saw the great 'classical' civilization of ancient Greece, and the rise of the Romans. These two civilizations had close links with other peoples, such as the Etruscans, Phoenicians and Carthaginians, who flourished around the shores of the warm Mediterranean Sea. Further away from the sunny Mediterranean were Celts, Britons, Iberians and Scythians, and beyond their lands lived other peoples in the remote and cold northlands of Europe.

People often claim that the idea of 'Europe' as a distinct region with a common culture is a modern one. But it is clear that in the ancient world, people thought of Europe as a region, one of the three parts of the known world – the other two being Africa and Asia. The peoples living around the Mediterranean traded with each other, and with the civilizations of the Middle East, from which they took many ideas and customs. Some peoples had direct contact with one another through trade. Others dealt through a 'middle group', such as the Etruscans who bought goods from the Greeks and sold them on to other people in central Europe. The cold north and northwest of the continent were not easy for southerners to reach, since the mountains and plains of central Europe were barriers to land travel, and the ships of the ancient world were not big or strong enough to sail regularly beyond the Mediterranean into the stormy Atlantic Ocean. Contacts between the Mediterranean peoples and those of northern Europe were therefore few.

What we know about these times comes from the writings of Greeks and Romans, from modern archaeological finds such as tombs, and from the study of ancient languages and religions. The Greek historian Herodotus wrote of Europe as the cradle of freedom and the foe of Asian (meaning Persian) tyranny. This idea has influenced many people but the truth was more complicated. The classical civilizations provide us with much written evidence about ancient Europe, its literature, laws and other records. The 'fringe' civilizations left less evidence, but have their own stories and their own place in Europe's cultural and economic development. A true picture of Europe as it was in ancient times can help us to understand the Europe of later centuries, and even the Europe of today.

In *The First Europeans* we see a Europe in which ancient peoples at different levels of culture mingled. The immeasurable contributions of the Greeks and the Eastern civilizations to Europe's development is clearly shown, but so also are the contributions of others, such as the Phoenicians, Romans and Celts.

In the period covered by this volume of THE ATLAS OF HUMAN HISTORY there was no central unifying force in Europe, like that later provided by the Roman Catholic Church. Different strands of development, from across the continent, were woven together to create the civilization we now call European. The maps and pictorial reconstructions illustrate this process, which is still going on today.

B.W.

CONTENTS

1 THE ACHAEANS

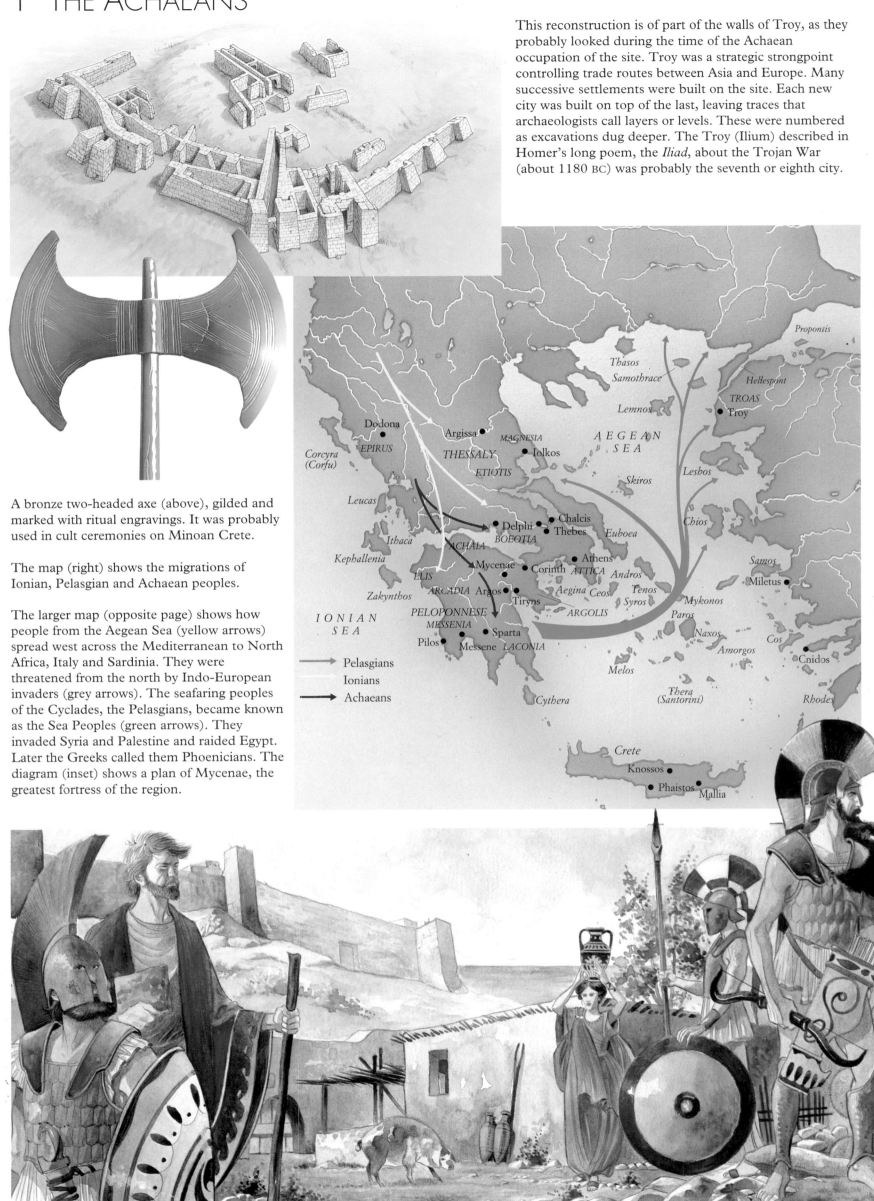

This reconstruction is of part of the walls of Troy, as they probably looked during the time of the Achaean occupation of the site. Troy was a strategic strongpoint controlling trade routes between Asia and Europe. Many successive settlements were built on the site. Each new city was built on top of the last, leaving traces that archaeologists call layers or levels. These were numbered as excavations dug deeper. The Troy (Ilium) described in Homer's long poem, the *Iliad*, about the Trojan War (about 1180 BC) was probably the seventh or eighth city.

A bronze two-headed axe (above), gilded and marked with ritual engravings. It was probably used in cult ceremonies on Minoan Crete.

The map (right) shows the migrations of Ionian, Pelasgian and Achaean peoples.

The larger map (opposite page) shows how people from the Aegean Sea (yellow arrows) spread west across the Mediterranean to North Africa, Italy and Sardinia. They were threatened from the north by Indo-European invaders (grey arrows). The seafaring peoples of the Cyclades, the Pelasgians, became known as the Sea Peoples (green arrows). They invaded Syria and Palestine and raided Egypt. Later the Greeks called them Phoenicians. The diagram (inset) shows a plan of Mycenae, the greatest fortress of the region.

→ Pelasgians
→ Ionians
→ Achaeans

The armies that attacked and finally destroyed Troy came from various Achaean kingdoms. The Achaeans lived in mainland Greece, Crete, Rhodes and other islands. They were noted for their military prowess, and some historians believe they were either Mycenaeans or soldiers in the service of the kings of Mycenae. In the *Iliad* Homer lists their ships, and commanders. The map (right) shows where Homer's Greeks reputedly came from.

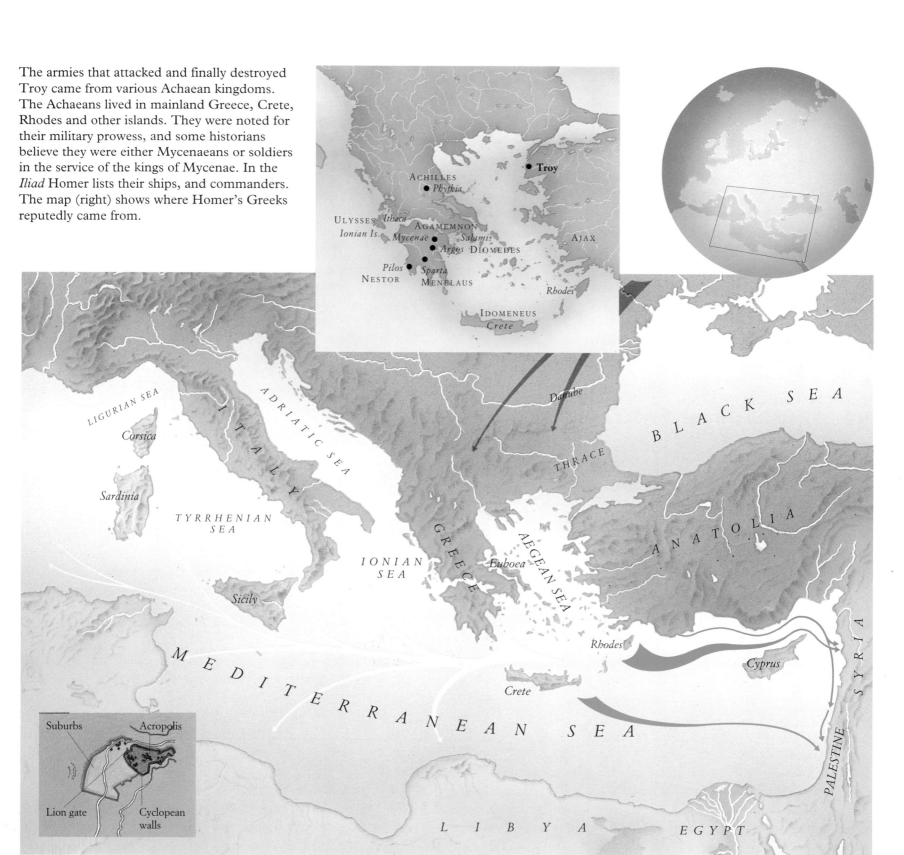

1 THE ACHAEANS

From the 1500s BC people who spoke Hellenic languages appeared throughout the Aegean Sea basin, on both the Greek and Anatolian (Turkish) sides of the sea. These people are usually called 'Achaeans'. They were warlike, owning horses and chariots, and fought with metal weapons. They moved considerable distances seeking new lands to settle and new peoples to enslave and dominate.

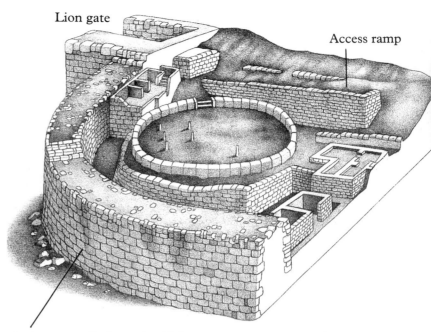

Cyclopean walls from the 13th century BC

Achaeans on the move

We know little about the Achaeans of Anatolia. The Hittites called them 'Ahhijawa'. But according to the traditional stories of the Greek historian Thucydides, the descendants of Pelops (from whom comes the name of the Peloponnesus region) had founded, around the 16th century BC, the Atrean dynasty of Mycenae. They then fought with other groups of peoples for control of the Greek peninsula.

The Achaeans spread into two settlement areas. One was west of the Aegean Sea, through Thessaly and Attica, and into the Peloponnese. The other was to the east, closer to Asia Minor and the surrounding islands. They were following the same routes as earlier Indo-European peoples who, at the end of the 3rd millennium, had come into the Aegean from the Black Sea region.

The Achaeans who first invaded the Greek mainland around 1900 BC were a rather backward group of soldiers and shepherds. Yet they were able to dominate the local people. Those who settled north of the isthmus of Corinth were known as Ionians, others as Danae (which meant 'navigators').

The Mycenaeans

The Achaean civilization came to be called 'Mycenaean', from its most famous centre, the fortress of Mycenae found in Argolis. It lasted for about 500 years, during which time the Mycenaean kings were buried amid treasures and

weapons in shaft tombs that have been excavated in modern times. There were other kingdoms, including Athens, Thebes, Orchomenos, Gla and Iolkos.

The Pelasgians, driven from their lands, founded new states on islands such as Lesbos and Chios. Others sought refuge in Thrace and Troas, where they mingled with the Phrygian peoples of Asia Minor. Many remained in Attica and Thessaly.

Achaean cities were almost always built in dominant positions, to control communication routes, and were defended by massive stone walls and ramparts. Wars between rival kings were recorded in legends, such as the stories of the struggle between Mycenae and the city of Thebes, which was destroyed about 1300 BC.

What we know of Mycenaean life

Information about the society, government and economy of the Mycenaean states is gathered from about 4,000 tablets

The scene (shown in colour on pages 4/5) shows people outside the walls of a Greek fortified city. Mycenaean fortresses were protected by massive stone walls. The Achaeans built similar strongholds to guard their coasts. These fortress-cities were among the most formidable strongholds of the ancient world.

The Achaeans may have been

unused to the sea when they first entered Greece, but they soon became expert sailors. They combined trading voyages with war raids and piracy.

In the background two ships approach the harbour. Other vessels are being unloaded. A woman carries a decorated pot on her head. The man (far left) is

perhaps a merchant or record-keeper; he carries a wax tablet.

The warriors wear armour, with plumed helmets and round shields. One carries a bow, with a quiver of arrows slung from his belt. Swords and spears are made of bronze.

On the right is a chariot pulled by two horses. Behind it is a cart, used for carrying farm produce or

booty brought home by warriors from a seaborne raid.

The wars of these people were immortalized by Greek writers into heroic contests, but the real struggles had more to do with control of trade, a vital route, market or area of influence. Trade and riches, rather than territory, were what Achaean kings and nobles coveted.

This reconstruction (left) is of part of the sacred tomb area of Mycenae. Mycenaean kings were buried in tombs dug in the rocks. The fortress walls were made of gigantic stones, called 'Cyclopean', because they were so heavy. According to legend the giant Cyclopes helped the builders put them in place.

Theseus and his companions leave their ship (right). This picture of Greek warrior-heroes, immortalized in stories, comes from a 6th-century vase found in an Etruscan tomb at Chiusi in Italy. It is now in the Archaeological Museum, Florence.

written in a script called 'Linear B'. Most of these were discovered at Knossos, on the island of Crete, and in Pilos.

From these writings we learn that the lord of the palace was known as the *wanaz*, and this title evidently carried a religious as well as a military significance. The name *basileus*, meaning 'king', was used only for governors and local leaders. The chief official was the *lawagetas*, or 'people's guide', possibly the supreme commander of the army.

The economy of the Mycenaean states seems to have been highly organized, governed by a strong central power, particularly from around 1500 BC, when the Cretans superseded the Achaeans as the most powerful traders. At this time, the ships of the Mycenaeans explored the Tyrrhenian Sea as far as the Aeolian Islands, Sicily and the shores of Italy. Although the Achaeans did not set up permanent settlements, their trade goods had a cultural influence on the peoples they met.

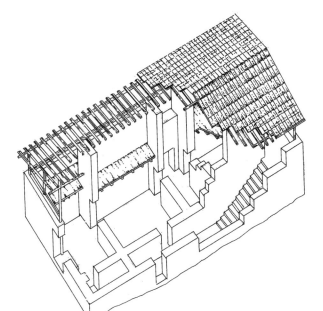

A reconstruction of a house from Kolona, Aegina. It is a typical Bronze Age dwelling from early Greece, with a staircase and a tiled roof.

Rise and fall of Mycenaean power
In the Aegean Sea, Mycenaean expansion resulted in the occupation of the scattered Ionian islands, the Cyclades Islands and Rhodes. Around 1450 BC Crete itself, the centre of Minoan power, was invaded. Later, sometime before 1150 BC, a major political event occurred – the combining of the Ahhijawa kingdom of Asia Minor (the eastern Achaeans) with their western cousins, the peoples of the Greek peninsula and islands, with their centre at Mycenae. The Aegean Sea was thenceforth an 'Achaean lake', particularly after the destruction of the rival power of Troy (about 1230 BC), and the occupation of the kingdom of Troas which controlled the sea routes in that region.

The end for the Achaeans was not sudden collapse but slow decline. The Sea Peoples' incursions made Crete and Cyprus independent trade centres, blocking the routes and markets used by Mycenae. Capturing Troy and its routes north to the Black Sea and northern Anatolia did not balance the loss of the valuable eastern outlets. The Greeks could not sell their goods as profitably as before, and this caused a crisis, leading to the end of Mycenaean power.

This painted vase (left) is in the stylized form of a woman holding a baby. It comes from a child's tomb in Mycenae dating from the 14th century BC.

A battle scene, from a vase, shows a Greek soldier with a shield and spear. Beside him in the chariot stands the goddess Athene, whom the Greeks believed protected them.

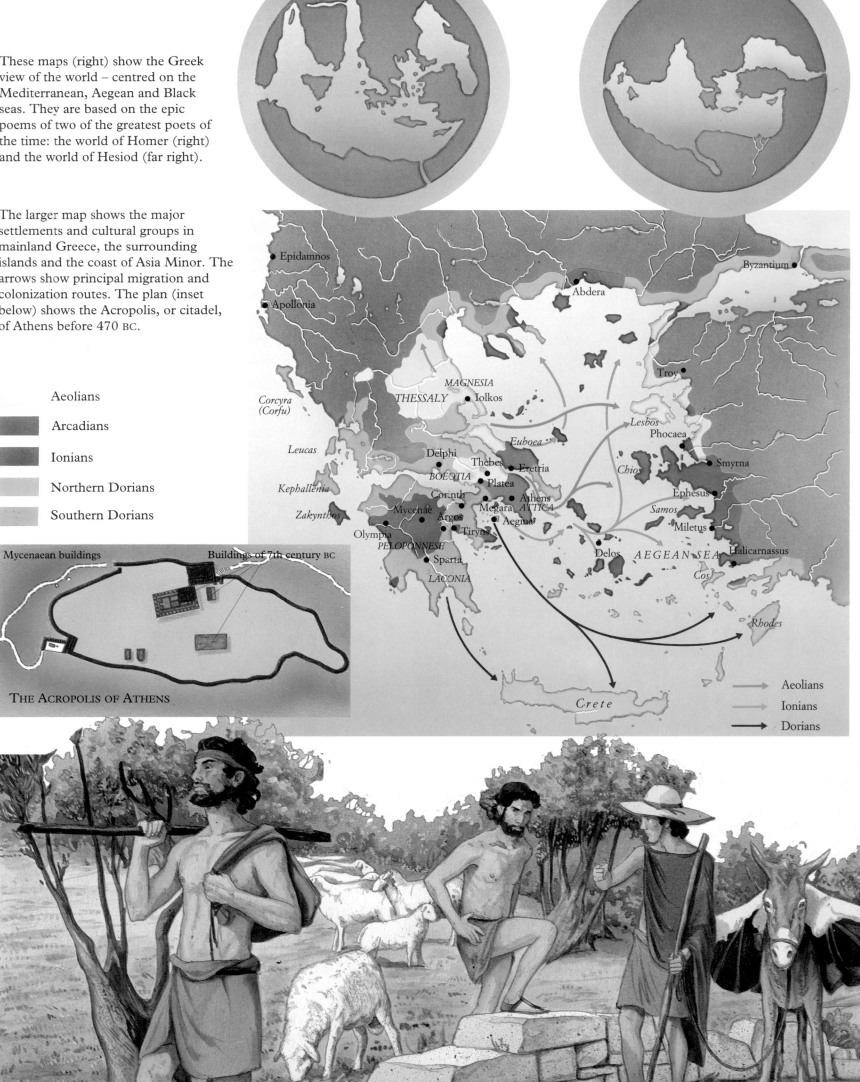

These maps (right) show the Greek view of the world – centred on the Mediterranean, Aegean and Black seas. They are based on the epic poems of two of the greatest poets of the time: the world of Homer (right) and the world of Hesiod (far right).

The larger map shows the major settlements and cultural groups in mainland Greece, the surrounding islands and the coast of Asia Minor. The arrows show principal migration and colonization routes. The plan (inset below) shows the Acropolis, or citadel, of Athens before 470 BC.

Aeolians

Arcadians

Ionians

Northern Dorians

Southern Dorians

Mycenaean buildings   Buildings of 7th century BC

THE ACROPOLIS OF ATHENS

Epidamnos

Byzantium

Apollonia

Abdera

Troy

MAGNESIA

THESSALY   Iolkos

Corcyra (Corfu)

Lesbos

Phocaea

Leucas

Euboea

Delphi

Thebes   Eretria

Smyrna

Chios

Kephallenia

BOEOTIA   Platea

Corinth   Athens   Ephesus

Zakynthos   Megara   ATTICA   Samos

Mycenae   Argos   Aegina   Miletus

Olympia   Tiryns   Delos   AEGEAN SEA   Halicarnassus

PELOPONNESE

Sparta   Cos

LACONIA   Rhodes

Crete

→ Aeolians

→ Ionians

→ Dorians

8

The map below shows the main Greek cities founded as colonies abroad. Each group of colonists comprised citizens from a *polis*, or city-state, who left their home city because of overcrowding, or to escape from new waves of immigrants. Colonists settled on favoured trade routes, or in places that offered good farmland or pasture for grazing animals. In their colonies, they planted their social organization, customs and religions. Many of these new cities soon became so prosperous that they overtook their home cities in importance. Syracuse and Agrigento in Sicily, Tarentum in southern Italy, and Ephesus and Miletus on the Aegean coast of Asia Minor are all good examples of colony-cities. The Greeks of southern Italy flourished to such an extent that their colony was given the name 'Great Greece'.

■ homeland cities   ▲ Achaean colonies   ◻ Dorian colonies   ○ Ionian colonies   ● other cities

9

2 THE ARCHAIC AGE IN GREECE

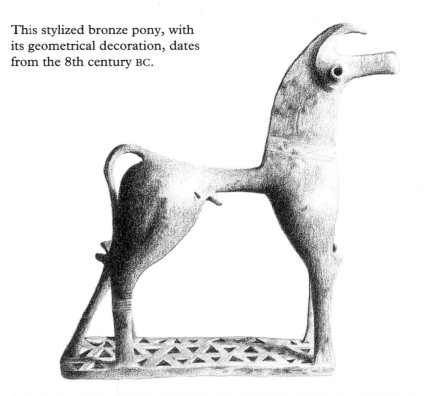

This stylized bronze pony, with its geometrical decoration, dates from the 8th century BC.

In the 12th century BC the Mycenaean kings gradually lost their power. The rise of the Sea Peoples, in the eastern Mediterranean, reduced the trade between the Achaean communities of Greece and the East. There were family feuds between Mycenaean rulers, a war against Thebes, and there is evidence of other violence from traces of fires and raids over much of the Greek world. The Achaeans were losing control.

The Dorian invasions
Into this turmoil came the Dorians, who seem to have been a people from the north and northwest of Greece. Their arrival did not cause a dramatic turnabout in the Greek way of life, for they shared many traditions. But the Mycenaean centres were weakened and destroyed, and the Dorians established themselves in Laconia, forming a new privileged military élite and replacing the old Mycenaean nobility.

Drought and famine may have played a part in these upheavals. It seems that populations scattered, and only a few places, such as Athens, remained as prosperous as before. To some historians, this period as the Bronze Age came to an end seems a Greek 'dark age'. Some Greeks from the mainland voyaged east to settle on the islands and coast of the eastern Aegean Sea in Asia Minor.

This coast included towns, such as Phocaea, Smyrna, Ephesus, Miletus and Halicarnassus, which were an integral part of the Greek world, and for some time the main centres of economic, civil and cultural development. The islands of Lesbos, Chios, Samos and Cos were also important settlement areas. Dorians went to the larger islands of Crete and Rhodes.

The Archaic period
The period of Greek history that historians call 'Archaic' begins roughly in the 8th century BC. By then there were three main groups of Greek peoples, identified by language differences. They were Aeolians, Ionians and Dorians, and they lived on both sides of the Aegean Sea. In some once-thriving cities, such as Corinth and Megara, the decline in local economies forced people to take up seafaring and foreign trade for the first time. The Greeks were now in a better position to compete with the powerful Phoenician traders and seafarers, since – after the defeat of Troy – they controlled the Aegean as far north as the entrance to the Black Sea.

Government in the city-state
Each state in Greece was organized according to local tradition, resulting in the fragmentation of the region into numerous self-governing city-states. These states were defined not by geographical boundaries, but by the

The scene (shown in colour on pages 8/9) shows farm workers tending olive trees. A cart pulled by donkeys waits to collect the harvest. The traveller (possibly a pedlar) also uses a donkey to carry his wares.

In the background is the hilltop acropolis where a new temple is being built. The god whom it honours will protect the people of the town, whose houses cluster below.

In ancient Greece, pastoral occupations – farming and herding – were thought the most appropriate activities to promote human dignity. Poets such as Hesiod wrote that farming made life possible and tolerable, even if it did not bring wealth.

Greece is a mountainous country, with relatively small areas of fertile farmland. Some farms were large estates owned by nobles, and left as grazing for sheep and goats. But most were small, and farmed by families, with perhaps one or two slaves to help with the work. Though regarded as the birthplace of Western democracy, Greece depended on slaves to keep its economy going.

The farmer aimed to feed his family from the produce of his own land, acquiring from others only things like salt and metals that he could not farm.

This picture of wrestlers (left) is geometric in style. Puzzlingly, each is shown grabbing his own hair. This motif recurs in vase decoration, and is known as far back as a fresco found on the island of Thera, from 1500 BC.

This small clay model of a temple (right) was found among votive offerings at the shrine of Hera, queen of the gods, at Peracora. It dates from 800 BC. The temple appears to have one large chamber, covered with a sloped thatched roof, and with a portico supported by columns.

common customs of their people, who agreed to accept the laws and religious practices of the state.

In time, the nobles regained their old ascendancy. The religious authority of ancient kingly power passed to an assembly of elders, made up of the heads of the oldest and most powerful land-owning families. This type of government is known as aristocracy.

In Athens, which according to tradition had a king until the 10th century BC, and in many other states of central Greece, the monarchy gradually lost its privileges. It was replaced by three *archons*, or magistrates, whose term of office was originally for life, then for ten years, and finally for a year only. In some states such as Corinth and Samos, nobles ruled in this manner. In others, there were still kings.

Citizen-soldiers and colonies

Midway through the 8th century BC there were aristocratic governments throughout most of the Greek world. However, over the next three hundred years there were important changes. Manufacturing increased, and so did seaborne trade. The army was reformed, allowing every free citizen able to arm himself at his own expense to become a soldier. These changes brought pressure on the ruling class from both merchants and craftworkers, and even from the mass of the people (known in Greek as *demos*). Ordinary citizens began to take part in politics, and there was a general acceptance that the laws of the state applied to all.

In spite of the number and diversity of city-states throughout Greece in the Archaic period, Greek life still showed a remarkable community of thought, custom and belief. The Greeks embarked on a second wave of colonization during the 8th-6th centuries BC, taking their ideas about the *polis*, or city-state, their laws, and their gods to other parts of the Mediterranean and Aegean coast. Unity of culture made the Greeks a more formidable force in the region, better able to fight against powerful foes, as they did in the great wars with Persia.

The owl, a bird held sacred to the goddess Athene, was adopted as the symbol of Attica. It appears on coins, like this one (above).

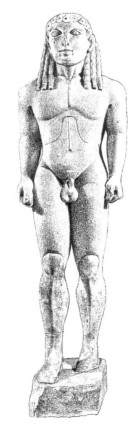

A bronze statue (above) of a Spartan soldier, from around 500 BC. He is wrapped in a cloak and wearing a helmet with a side-to-side crest. Sparta was a city-state in Laconia, where the Dorians settled. The Spartans developed a militaristic society.

Cleobis was one of two legendary brothers from Argos. His statue (right) is now in the Delphi Museum. It was a votive offering, in thanks for the gods' aid.

3 GODS AND MYTHS OF THE GREEK WORLD

This picture (right) from a red-painted vase shows the hero Hercules (Herakles) wearing the skin of a lion. He is struggling with the god Apollo. In one of his many adventures, Hercules stole the sacred tripod of the Pythia, the woman who spoke the prophecies of the oracle at Delphi. This angered Apollo, and Hercules was eventually condemned to a year's slavery.

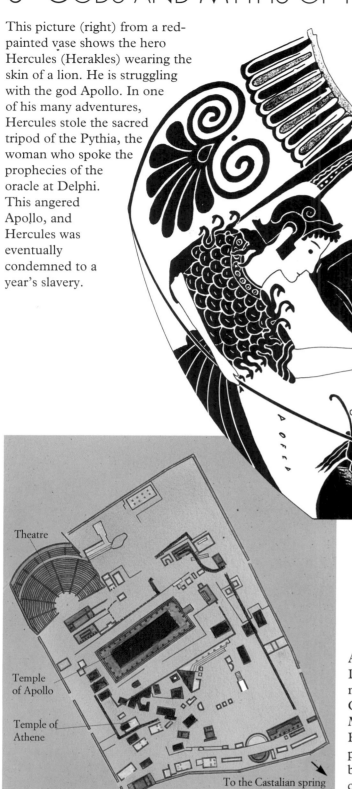

A plan of the oracle at Delphi (left). This was the most famous oracle in Greece, on the slopes of Mount Parnassus. Buildings from the Archaic period are in red, those belonging to Panhellenic cults are in yellow.

Theatre

Temple of Apollo

Temple of Athene

To the Castalian spring

The map (right) shows the chief shrines, oracles and other sacred places of the Olympian gods of the ancient Greek world. According to the historian Herodotus, the most important oracles were at Delphi, Dodona and Siwa (an oasis in Libya, then part of Egypt). There were also others of less importance. People came to the oracles and other holy places, usually on mountains, to consult the gods through a priestess or medium. Shrines were dedicated to various gods, the chief of whom was Zeus.

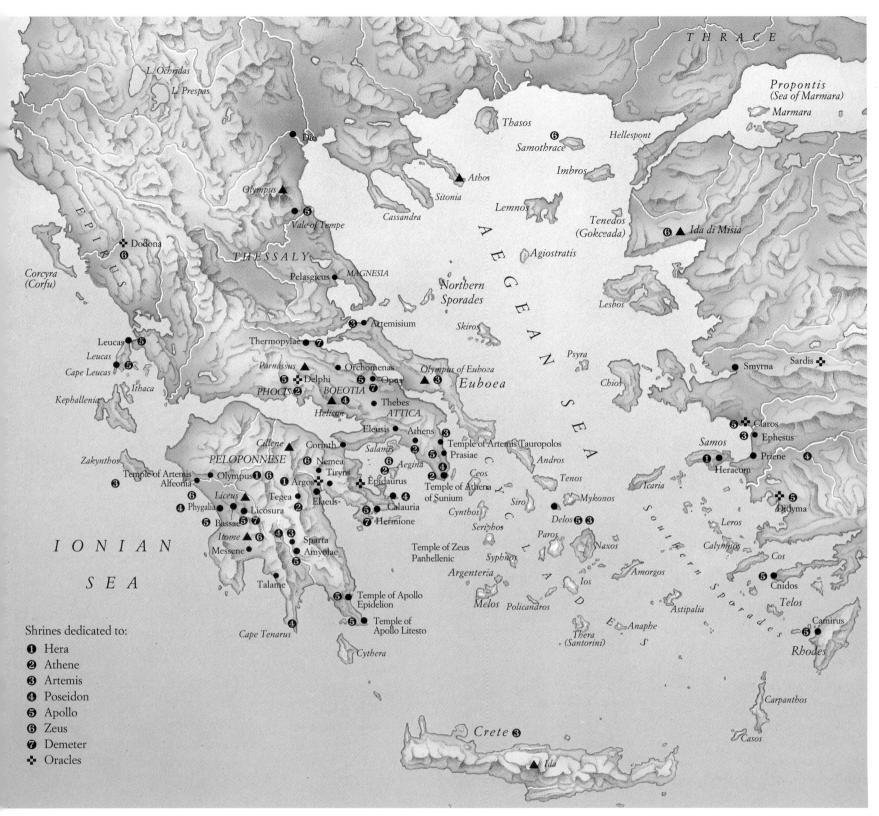

Shrines dedicated to:

❶ Hera
❷ Athene
❸ Artemis
❹ Poseidon
❺ Apollo
❻ Zeus
❼ Demeter
✚ Oracles

THRACE

Propontis (Sea of Marmara)
Marmara

L. Ochridas
L. Prespas

Dio
Thasos
Samothrace ❻
Hellespont

Olympus ▲
Athos ▲
Imbros

Sitonia
❺ *Vale of Tempe*
Cassandra
Lemnos
Tenedos (Gokceada)
❻ ▲ *Ida di Misia*

EPIRUS
Corcyra (Corfu)
✚ Dodona ❻
THESSALY
Pelasgicus ● MAGNESIA
Agiostratis
Lesbos

Northern Sporades
AEGEAN SEA

Smyrna
Sardis ✚

❸ Artemisium
Skiros
Psyra
Chios

Leucas ❺
Leucas
Cape Leucas ❺
Ithaca
Kephallenia

Thermopylae ❼
Parnassus ▲ ● Orchomenas
❺ ✚ Delphi ● Opus ❼
PHOCIS ❷ BOEOTIA
Helicon ● ❹
Olympus of Euboea ▲ ❸
Euboea

❺ Claros
Ephesus
Samos
Priene ❹

Zakynthos
Temple of Artemis Alfeonia
❻
Cillene ▲
Corinth
Salamis
Eleusis ● Athens ❸
Temple of Artemis Tauropolos
Andros
❶ Heraeum
Didyma ✚ ❺
Leros

PELOPONNESE
❸ Olympus ❶
Nemea ❻
❶ Argos
Tiryns
Aegina ❻
❷
❹ Prasiae
Ceos
Tenos
Icaria
Calynmos

Liceus ❻ ▲
Tegea
Elaeus ✚
Epidaurus
❹ Calauria
Temple of Athena of Sunium
Cynthos
Siro
Mykonos
Delos ❺ ❸
Cos
Cnidos ❺
Telos

Phygalia ❹
Licosura
Bassae ❺
Itome ▲ ❻
Messene
❷
❸
Sparta
Amyclae
Hermione ❼
Temple of Zeus Panhellenic
Seriphos
Syphnos
Paros
Naxos
Amorgos
Southern Sporades
Camirus
❺

IONIAN SEA
Talame
Temple of Apollo Epidelion ❺
Temple of Apollo Litesto ❺
Cape Tenarus ❹
Cythera
Argenteria
Melos
Policandros
Ios
Anaphe
Thera (Santorini)
Astipalia
CYCLADES
Rhodes
Carpanthos
Casos

Crete ❸
Ida ▲

3 GODS AND MYTHS OF THE GREEK WORLD

This bronze statue of Apollo comes from Piraeus, and dates from the end of the 6th century BC. Originally the figure held a bow in its left hand, and a bowl for offerings in the right.

The Greeks founded sanctuaries and shrines dedicated to their chief gods throughout the areas they settled. Many of these temples became centres for cults, dedicated to particular gods, that spread and attained a greater importance in the wider area of Greek influence known as the Panhellenic world. The god's sanctuary became a meeting place for religious, political and social purposes.

The Gods of Olympus

The gods of Greece were based on Mount Olympus. There were 12 great gods and goddesses: Zeus, Poseidon, Hephaestus, Hermes, Ares, Apollo (male) and Hera, Athene, Artemis, Hestia, Aphrodite and Demeter (female). There were other lesser gods and also mortals with superhuman powers, known as heroes.

Shrines and oracles

For Ionian Greeks, the most venerated sanctuaries were the shrines of Poseidon at Mycale in Asia Minor and of Apollo at Delos. For Dorian Greeks the shrines of Apollo at Cnidus in Asia Minor and of Poseidon at Calauria had especial importance. The cults of Zeus attracted wider Panhellenic devotion, and the god had important shrines at Olympia, Elis and Dodona. Apollo was especially important because he was the god of divination and prophecy.

The oracle at Delphi

People came to the oracle at Delphi to hear the prophecies of the priestess, or Pythia, who (they believed) was inspired by Apollo. Delphi was the oracle that people throughout the Greek world venerated. It was the centre of a cult-group, or league, made up of various Greek peoples, including Thessalians, Boeotians, Dorians, Ionians and Phocians. They came together to look after the oracle and maintain its temple.

The Delphi league came into being when followers of the cult of Demeter (goddess of harvests) joined with the followers of Apollo at Delphi, perhaps at the end of the 7th century BC. The contrasts between the different people sharing the Apollo cult is symbolized in the story of the struggle between Apollo and Hercules. Hercules was not a god, but a hero – a mortal person who could mix with the gods, and whose powers were greater than those of ordinary beings. Thebes and Argos were the centres of Hercules' fame, but like Apollo, he was venerated throughout the Greek world.

The picture (in colour on pages 12/13) shows the oracle at Delphi, the greatest of all Greek oracles. A suitable place for one of these mysterious shrines was a natural spring, a wood containing a mountain landslip, or a ravine or gorge which gave a distorted echo.

The oracle site was within a sacred circle, maintained by local people. If the god showed his appreciation of people's offerings, a temple or temples were built. At Delphi steam rose from a cleft in the ground. The oracle was dedicated to Apollo. It was at Delphi, according to the story, that Apollo fought and slew the serpent-monster Python.

The Pythia, the priestess of the oracle, sat on a tripod, or three-legged stool. In a state of trance, and shrouded in steam, she replied to questioners in obscure and ambiguous words. Her replies were interpreted by priests attending her.

The fame of this oracle spread throughout the ancient world.

Kings, ambassadors from foreign states, and ordinary citizens waited for the Pythia to give her inspired replies to their questions – which might range from everyday concerns to matters of state such as the conduct of a war, whether to maintain or break an alliance, and where to found a new colony.

A statue of Athene Parthenos (left) as a warrior goddess. In other guises Athene was also goddess of the arts of peace and of wisdom. Athene was especially venerated in Athens.

Hermes (left) was the messenger of the gods. He was also the god of travellers and trade. On this coin from the late 6th century BC, he is shown fastening his winged sandals.

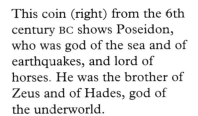

This coin (right) from the 6th century BC shows Poseidon, who was god of the sea and of earthquakes, and lord of horses. He was the brother of Zeus and of Hades, god of the underworld.

Holy wars and treasures

The league ran the oracle site, took care of the offerings brought to the god, made sure the sacred ground was not tampered with (by farmers planting crops), and looked after the roads leading to the site. It also punished people who broke the rules, by imposing fines or exile, or even by making war upon them.

There were in fact four serious conflicts for control of the Delphi oracle, for this was more than a religious shrine, it was a political centre, for people from all over the Greek world. It was an ideal stage for propaganda, either through the oracle or through other activities such as dedications, athletic games, and proclamations made at festivals. The so-called Pythic festival was held every four years.

Making the oracle work for you

Politicians and leaders used Delphi as a law-making centre, and the oracle was frequently consulted during major crises and discussions of events. The course of Greek history often depended on which party controlled the oracle – sometimes the Thessalians, sometimes the Athenians or Spartans, and so on.

At times important historical consequences followed from interpretations of the oracle. For example, the failure of the oracle's attempt to discourage Greek resistance in the imminent war with Persia resulted in a heavy blow to the oracle's authority.

The shrines and sanctuaries became treasuries, for people deposited valuables at them as offerings. Delphi represented a 'bank' of immense wealth for a country like Greece which had few mineral resources or precious metals. Consequently oracle sites were attractive to greedy tyrants. Dionysus of Syracuse, one such tyrant, plundered the sacred sanctuaries of western Greece when he needed money.

Divine riddles and healing dreams

Oracles (whether dedicated to Zeus, Apollo or some other god) provided direct communication to the deities in various ways. At some oracles a priest-prophet gave out complex coded messages (this was how the Pythia at Delphi gave her prophecies). At others the petitioner slept in the oracle sanctuary and dreamed the divine message.

Health shrines dedicated to gods of healing became very popular. The sanctuary of Asclepius at Epidaurus was visited by sick people from all over Greece; here the dream-technique was used to effect cures. Grateful pilgrims left offerings to the healer god, and many such gifts have been found by archaeologists.

This engraved bronze mirror shows Aphrodite (goddess of love, and probably of Eastern origin) playing dice with Pan.

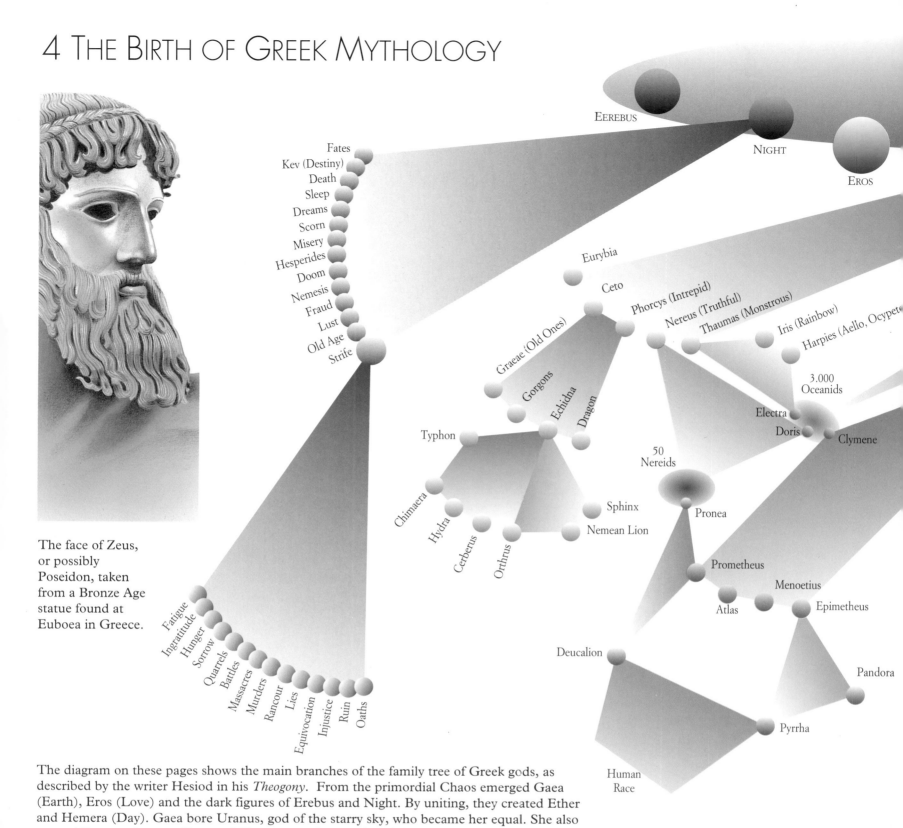

The face of Zeus, or possibly Poseidon, taken from a Bronze Age statue found at Euboea in Greece.

EEREBUS

NIGHT

EROS

Fates
Kev (Destiny)
Death
Sleep
Dreams
Scorn
Misery
Hesperides
Doom
Nemesis
Fraud
Lust
Old Age
Strife

Fatigue
Ingratitude
Hunger
Sorrow
Quarrels
Battles
Massacres
Murders
Rancour
Lies
Equivocation
Injustice
Ruin
Oaths

Eurybia
Ceto
Phorcys (Intrepid)
Nereus (Truthful)
Thaumas (Monstrous)
Iris (Rainbow)
Harpies (Aello, Ocypete

Graeae (Old Ones)
Gorgons
Echidna
Dragon

Typhon

Chimaera
Hydra
Cerberus
Orthus

Sphinx
Nemean Lion

3.000
Oceanids

Electra
Doris
Clymene

50
Nereids

Pronea

Prometheus

Menoetius

Atlas
Epimetheus

Deucalion

Pandora

Pyrrha

Human
Race

The diagram on these pages shows the main branches of the family tree of Greek gods, as described by the writer Hesiod in his *Theogony*. From the primordial Chaos emerged Gaea (Earth), Eros (Love) and the dark figures of Erebus and Night. By uniting, they created Ether and Hemera (Day). Gaea bore Uranus, god of the starry sky, who became her equal. She also created Pontus, the sea. Gaea and Uranus together produced the Titans, the first race of gods. They also produced three giant Cyclopes, and three monsters known as the Hecatonchoeires.

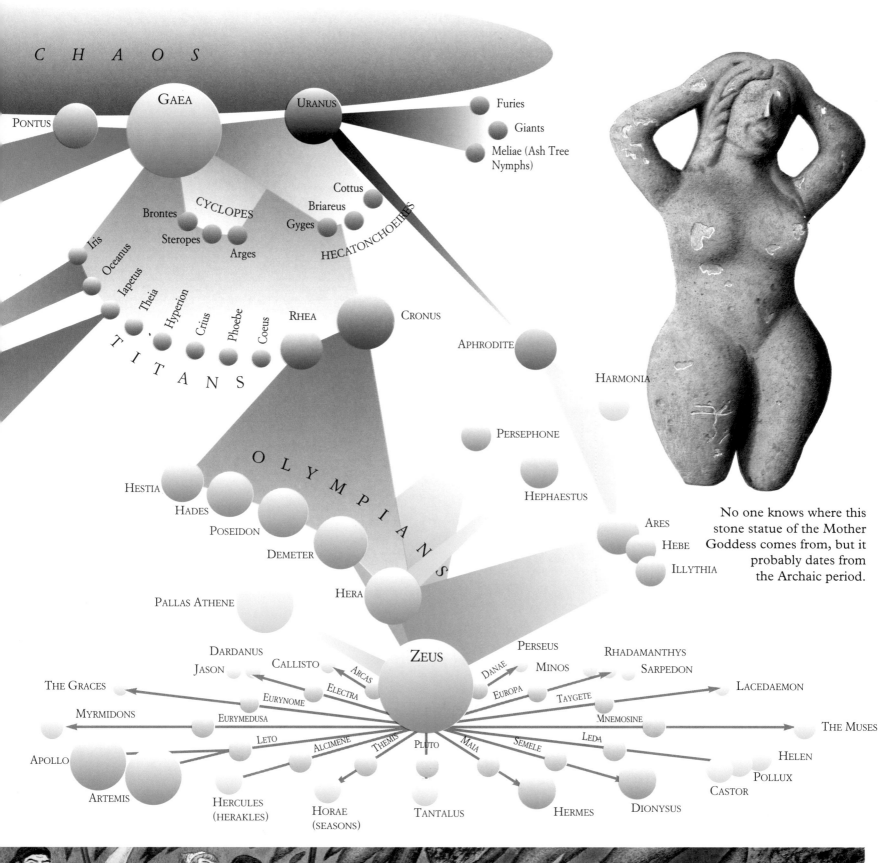

CHAOS

PONTUS

GAEA

URANUS

Furies

Giants

Meliae (Ash Tree Nymphs)

Cottus

Briareus

Gyges

HECATONCHOEIRES

CYCLOPES

Brontes

Steropes

Arges

Iris

Oceanus

Iapetus

Theia

Hyperion

Crius

Phoebe

Coeus

RHEA

CRONUS

APHRODITE

HARMONIA

TITANS

PERSEPHONE

HEPHAESTUS

OLYMPIANS

HESTIA

HADES

POSEIDON

DEMETER

HERA

ARES

HEBE

ILLYTHIA

No one knows where this stone statue of the Mother Goddess comes from, but it probably dates from the Archaic period.

PALLAS ATHENE

ZEUS

DARDANUS

CALLISTO

ARCAS

JASON

ELECTRA

EURYNOME

EURYMEDUSA

LETO

ALCIMENE

THEMIS

PLUTO

MAIA

SEMELE

LEDA

MNEMOSINE

PERSEUS

DANAE

MINOS

EUROPA

TAYGETE

RHADAMANTHYS

SARPEDON

LACEDAEMON

THE MUSES

THE GRACES

MYRMIDONS

APOLLO

ARTEMIS

HERCULES (HERAKLES)

HORAE (SEASONS)

TANTALUS

HERMES

DIONYSUS

CASTOR

POLLUX

HELEN

4 THE BIRTH OF GREEK MYTHOLOGY

The invaders and immigrants who arrived in the Aegean area from the end of the 3rd millennium brought with them different religious traditions and myths. The word 'myth' originally meant 'story' – one of sacred traditions. But the Greeks regarded myths as the truth, especially those that related the remote history and traditions of individual cities and their peoples, about which there was no actual evidence. The greatest influences came from the East, but also from Crete, North Africa, Egypt and Phoenicia. The ancient Aegean cult of the Mother Goddess survived alongside the male gods, among whom the leading role was given to Zeus, god of the sky and wild weather.

Local gods and cults

There was no one cult in Greek religion. Every city had its own gods and its own cults, derived from local tradition, which in turn drew on complex myths handed down usually by oral tradition (story-telling and poetry). It was not religion's role to know the nature of the gods or to determine the rules of human moral behaviour. This was more the preserve of philosophy. The sphere of religion was officially that of the state. The aim of its complex rites, sacrifices, prayers and dedications was to assure prosperity, by gaining the favour of the gods.

The Greek city-state was based on a community of cults and laws. The cult through which it honoured its protector gods (as, for example, Athene protected Athens) and its heroes (who were semi-divine, and often associated with the founding of a city) formed one of the community's unifying elements. Some cults became widespread, and were celebrated by all Greeks in large sanctuaries, such as that for Apollo at Delphi or for Zeus at Olympia. The frequent festivals held there were occasions for important meetings, between peoples who lived in a politically fragmented world, but were united by language and culture.

The creation of the gods

Foremost among the traditions which have preserved the main elements of Greek myth is Hesiod's *Theogony*. The title *Theogony* refers only to the birth of the gods, but

The picture (in colour on pages 16/17) shows the war between the Titans and the Olympians. In his account Hesiod describes how for ten years the Titans, male and female, fought the children of Rhea and Cronus, who remained steadfast on Mount Olympus. The Titans rebelled against the new Olympian gods, and launched an attack on Olympus from their own mountain, Othrys. On Gaea's advice Zeus recalled the three terrible and immensely strong Hecatonchoeires – fifty-headed monsters each with a hundred hands. He also had on his side the one-eyed giants, the Cyclopes, whose names meant thunder (Brontes), lightning (Steropes) and thunderbolt (Arges).

For the Greeks this battle was one of epic and terrible violence: 'The huge sea echoed terribly and the earth thundered while the heavens shook... Zeus, unable to contain his fury, hurled himself from the summit of Mount Olympus, and blinding flashes of lightning enveloped the Titans in a red-hot mist. The fire even reached Chaos.' Assailed by Zeus's fury, and by boulders hurled by the Hecatonchoeires, the Titans were finally defeated and buried deep below the surface of the earth.

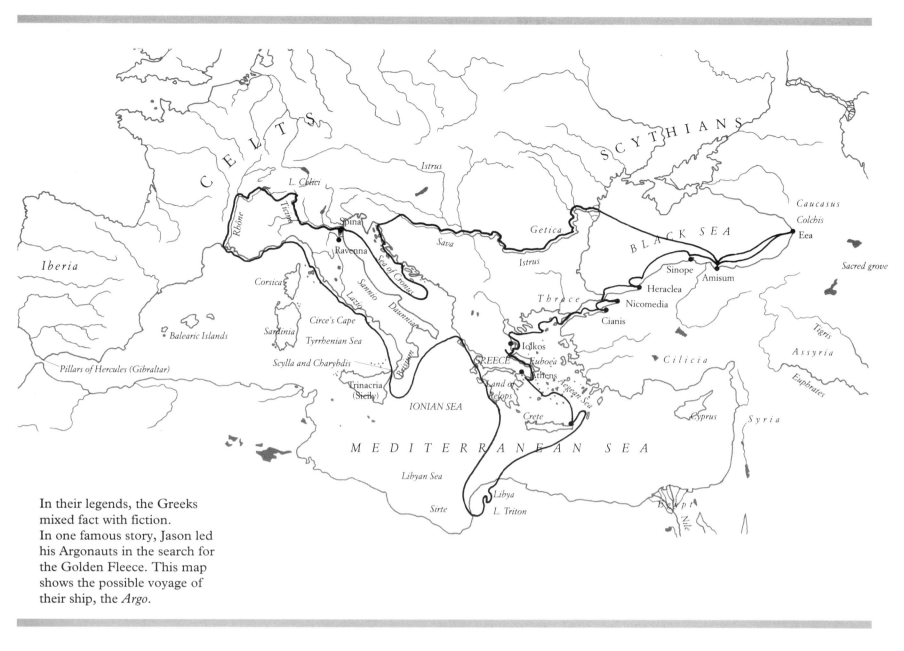

In their legends, the Greeks mixed fact with fiction. In one famous story, Jason led his Argonauts in the search for the Golden Fleece. This map shows the possible voyage of their ship, the *Argo*.

Hesiod's work is really a *cosmogony*, a story of the birth of the whole universe, including the creation of the gods.

In the beginning was Chaos (space). From Chaos, emerges Gaea (Earth). Then comes Eros, love and reproductive force; then Erebus and Night (darkness) and their opposites Ether and Day. Uranus, the starry sky, brings in a male element, to partner Gaea, the Earth Mother.

From the union of Gaea and Uranus are born the natural forces and features of the universe, such as mountains and seas, and also abstract concepts such as justice. This part of the *Theogony* shows a close relation to ancient Eastern cosmologies.

After the universe is formed and peopled by the Titans, Gaea urges her children to rebel against their father Uranus, who buries them deep in the earth. Cronus castrates his father Uranus, seizes power, and marries his sister Rhea. But he then swallows the children born of this union. Zeus escapes this fate and forces his father to regurgitate his brothers. He takes over as supreme head. After a series of family struggles, including the war against the Titans, Zeus becomes king of all the gods and order reigns throughout the universe.

From Zeus's many marriages are produced other gods and semi-gods, who complete the Olympian pantheon. It was thought by the Greeks that Zeus and his fellow gods lived on Olympus, the highest mountain in Greece.

Some aspects of this myth suggest a possible political interpretation. It is possible to recognize in Uranus and Cronus the old absolute rulers, defeated by the nobles, and replaced by a king who reigned supreme over the governing assembly. In this sense, the story seems to reflect ancient history in which Archaic Greece left the darkness – the Hellenic middle ages – for a new system of monarchy, which was to prove more stable and capable of collaboration through alliances.

The nature of the Greek gods

The Olympian religion had no real theology, and the nature of the gods was vaguely defined. Gods were immortal, immune from death, illness and worries of the kind that afflict people. They were powerful, within a realm of limited action, and like people, were conditioned by Fate.

Some gods were linked to the natural forces and the cosmos – such as Zeus or Poseidon. Others had a more intimate link with the earth, such as Demeter (fertility and harvest), or were tied to aspects of human behaviour, like Athene (wise virgin, warrior and often protector of cities). Their nature and actions are those of the human world, rather than a supernatural one.

Secret cults and mysteries

The Olympian religion, however, was not the only one practised in the Greek world. Other mysterious cults involved secret rites and promised the survival of a person's soul and eternal happiness – to which the Olympian religion paid little attention. One famous cult, known as the Eleusian Mysteries, centred on Demeter's search for her daughter Kore (Persephone).

The map of Central Europe (right) shows the main sites of Celtic-Hallstatt culture during the Iron Age.

This bronze ceremonial axe (below), with its mounted figure, comes from Hallstatt in Austria.

- Sites of early Hallstatt culture
▲ Sites of later Hallstatt culture

BRITISH ISLES

Thames

Frisian Islands

EARLY GERMANIC PEOPLES

Elbe

• Lovosice

English Channel

Rhine

Seine

• Gross Eibstadt

• Koberstadt

Main

U R N F I E L D   C U L T U R E S

▲ Bad Cannstatt

• Beilngries

• Gomadingen

Danube

▲ Vix
▲ Ste-Colombe

▲ Kappel am Rhein

▲ Heuneburg

▲ Apremont

▲ Villingen   • Mindelheim

L. Constance

Inn

Hallstatt •

Rhein

▲ Grachwil

Château-sur-Salins ▲

▲ Payerne

EARLY ITALI

L. Geneva

Sveta Lucija •

Ticino

Adda

L. Garda

Adige

Po

ADRIATIC SEA

Rhône

LIGURIAN SEA

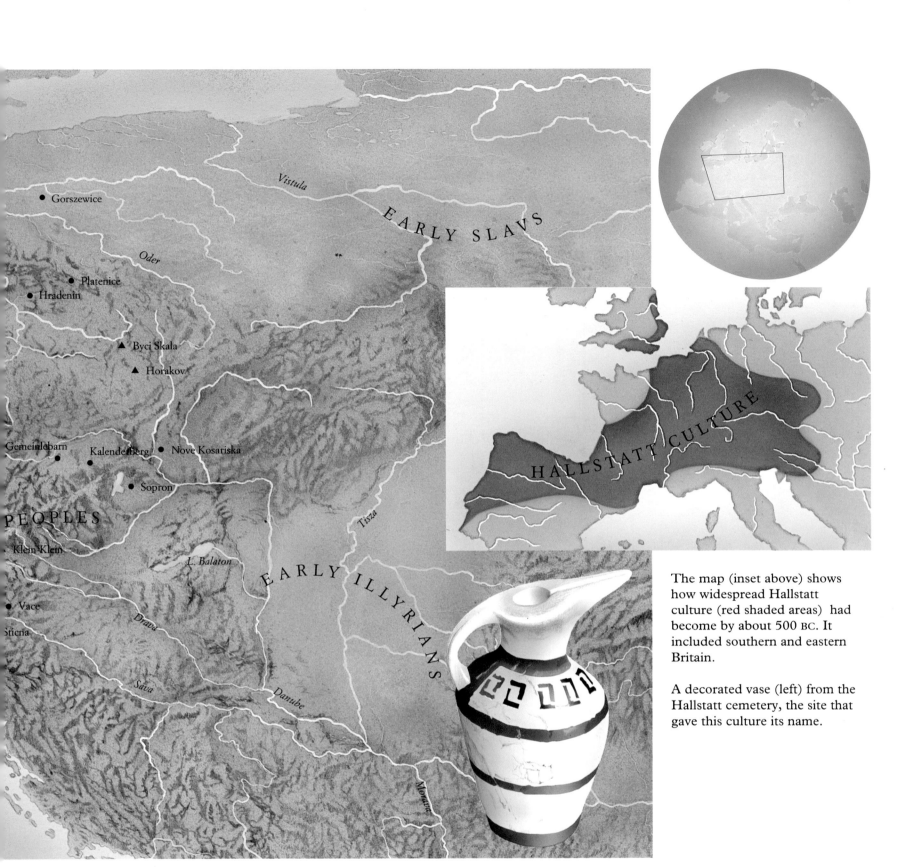

The map (inset above) shows how widespread Hallstatt culture (red shaded areas) had become by about 500 BC. It included southern and eastern Britain.

A decorated vase (left) from the Hallstatt cemetery, the site that gave this culture its name.

5 CENTRAL EUROPE IN THE BRONZE AND IRON AGES

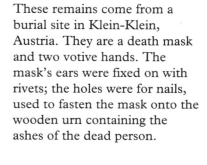

These remains come from a burial site in Klein-Klein, Austria. They are a death mask and two votive hands. The mask's ears were fixed on with rivets; the holes were for nails, used to fasten the mask onto the wooden urn containing the ashes of the dead person.

In mainland Europe, a marked growth in population in the early and middle Bronze Age (1700 to 1300 BC) was linked to an increase in farming production. Ploughing of fields was common, and traces of ploughed furrows have even been found under tombs in more northerly regions.

Trade routes across Europe

Bronze working of tools and weapons was widespread from Alsace (France) in the west to the Czech and Slovak regions in the east, and included the Alps and northern Germany. It was encouraged by trade between northern Europe (along the so-called Baltic amber route) and the eastern Mediterranean (Rhône-Rhine and Elbe-Brenner routes). Trading expeditions went to the British Isles, for tin, and also to the eastern Mediterranean, especially to the Aegean states, through the Danube river basin and the Black Sea. Goods then moved on into Greece and even Egypt.

In the 1200s BC, warlike peoples originating mainly from the Danube basin destroyed Mycenaean rule. Other population movements affected the tribes living between the Elbe and Vistula rivers, and in southern Germany along the rivers Rhône and Rhine.

Urnfield culture

From the end of the 1100s BC there was a more stable period. Typical of this time is the culture known as Urnfield, from the widespread funeral custom of burying the cremated ashes of the dead in urns in cemeteries. The most important Urnfield find has been at Unětice near Prague (Czech Republic). It corresponds to the final phase of the Bronze Age, during which a large mass of people was concentrated in central-western Europe.

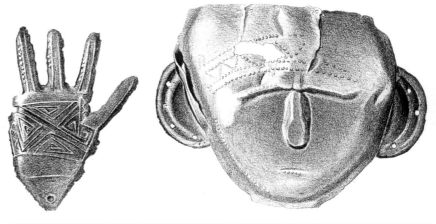

Hallstatt culture

The Iron Age culture which then emerged takes its name from the Hallstatt cemetery in upper Austria, where the first graves and iron tools made by these people were discovered. Hallstatt culture is found throughout Bosnia, Austria, southern Germany, Switzerland and north-central France. Fringe areas such as Slovakia, southern France and Spain were less well developed, and the Atlantic and Baltic coasts remained outside it.

Mining for salt and iron

Besides farming, the Hallstatt people had two main activities: they mined salt and iron ore. Salt was very important. As well as being used for flavouring cooked foods, it was also a preservative. Salted fish and meat would keep, to feed a family in winter or on a journey. The preservative quality of salt also helped the archaeologists, who excavated

The scene (pictured in colour on pages 20/21) shows a Hallstatt village. Farming still dominates people's lives. The soil is fertile, suitable for crops as well as grazing animals. People still hunt, and two men are bringing in a deer.

The people live in round houses with straw-thatch roofs. They use two-wheeled chariots (left) as well as heavier carts. Women weave cloth, and cook food over the central hearth.

Many settlements were near

rock salt mines. Rock salt was easier to extract than sea salt obtained by evaporating sea water.

At the edge of the village, close to the mine entrance, are wide shallow tanks. Into these, miners empty the concentrated rock salt, which is dissolved in water heated

by a fire to get rid of impurities.

The salt is then dried in the sun and, in the form of loaves or bricks, traded across Europe. The Hallstatt miners also found iron ore easy to reach, since it was near the surface. This gave them another valuable source of wealth.

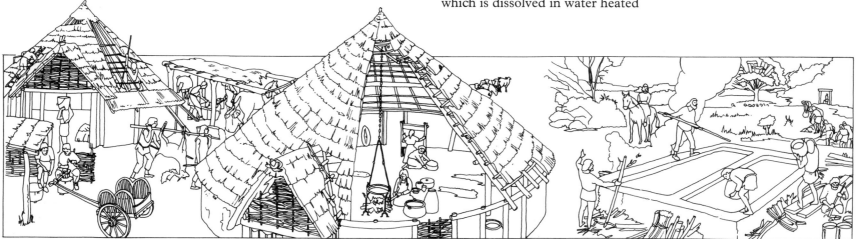

This clay statuette (left) of a man riding a horse comes from Bavaria, Germany.

This bronze statue of a female figure with raised hands comes from Austria.

This bronze cauldron (below), with its handle in the form of a calf, is also from Austria.

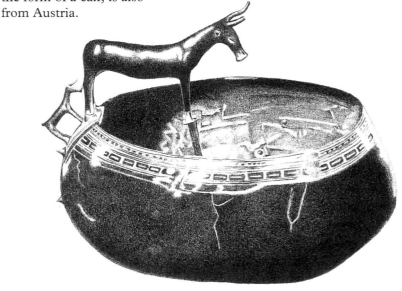

the Hallstatt cemetery near a salt mine, for here they found tools, clothes and even human bodies in a good state of preservation.

Throughout the 10th century BC, Hallstatt people learned to work iron as well as bronze. Compared to the Middle East and Anatolia, Europe was slow to adopt the use of iron. Knowledge of the new technology came along the salt-trade routes, with peoples like the Greeks and Etruscans, who knew about iron. Iron, however, was not an immediate substitute for bronze. Further technical discoveries were needed (the addition of carbon, for example) to make iron tools superior to bronze.

Controlling the trade

The Hallstatt people's world was ruled by a warring aristocracy that imposed itself on independent groups of farmers living in small settlements. Their power was based on the possession of weapons and also on their ownership of huge herds of cattle and sheep. Indeed, their military prowess may have been the result of having to guard these herds. The nobles also controlled trade, which became of major importance when the northern Mediterranean regions made contact with mainland Europe.

At points where trade routes met, such as Saxony and Thuringia (Germany), it was possible to control north-south and east-west routes at the same time. Here local warlords held sway, backed by fortified villages. Such places were of strategic and economic importance, being both markets and sorting centres for goods. Caravans of wagons with four iron-rimmed wheels passed through them, across the Rhône and the Alpine passes. They carried Cornish tin, gold from the Rhineland and Bohemia, amber from the Baltic, slaves and furs from the Scythian steppes, and fabric, pottery, luxury goods and wine from the Mediterranean southlands.

The prosperity and splendour of the Hallstatt nobility is revealed by the wealth of their tombs. In these tombs, wagon harnesses, brooches, necklaces, belts, hairpins and other personal ornaments have been found.

These rock engravings (below) come from Val Fontanalba in Italy. They show warriors displaying symbolic weapons (axes?) – presumably meant to impress visiting traders.

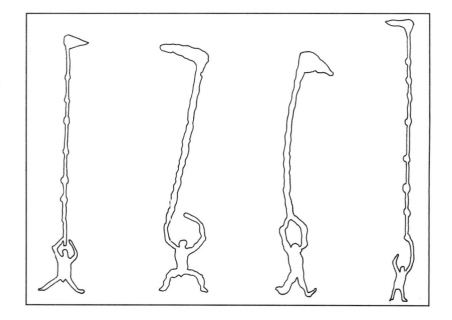

The map shows sites where archaeologists have made finds from the Bronze Age in Scandinavia. It also shows the main routes for trading amber, from the main sources (shaded).

Redrawn from a rock painting, this picture (below) is probably of a dancer in ceremonial costume. It comes from Järrestad in Sweden.

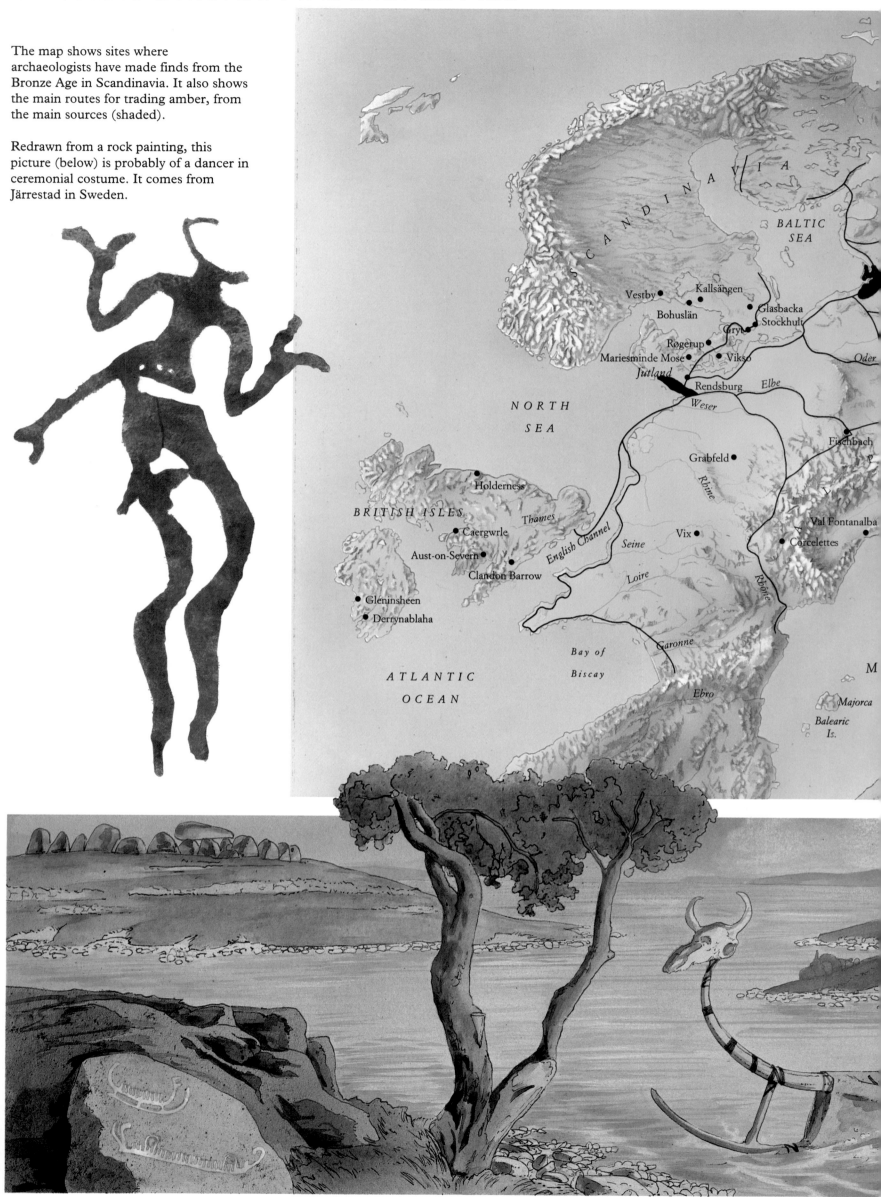

SCANDINAVIA

BALTIC SEA

Vestby

Kallsängen

Bohuslän

Glasbacka
Stockhult

Gryt

Røgerup

Mariesminde Mose

Viksø

Jutland

Rendsburg

Elbe

Oder

Weser

NORTH SEA

Fischbach

Grabfeld

Rhine

Holderness

BRITISH ISLES

Thames

Caergwrle

Vix

Val Fontanalba

Aust-on-Severn

English Channel

Seine

Corcelettes

Clandon Barrow

Loire

Gleninsheen

Rhône

Derrynablaha

Bay of Biscay

Garonne

ATLANTIC OCEAN

Ebro

Majorca

Balearic Is.

M

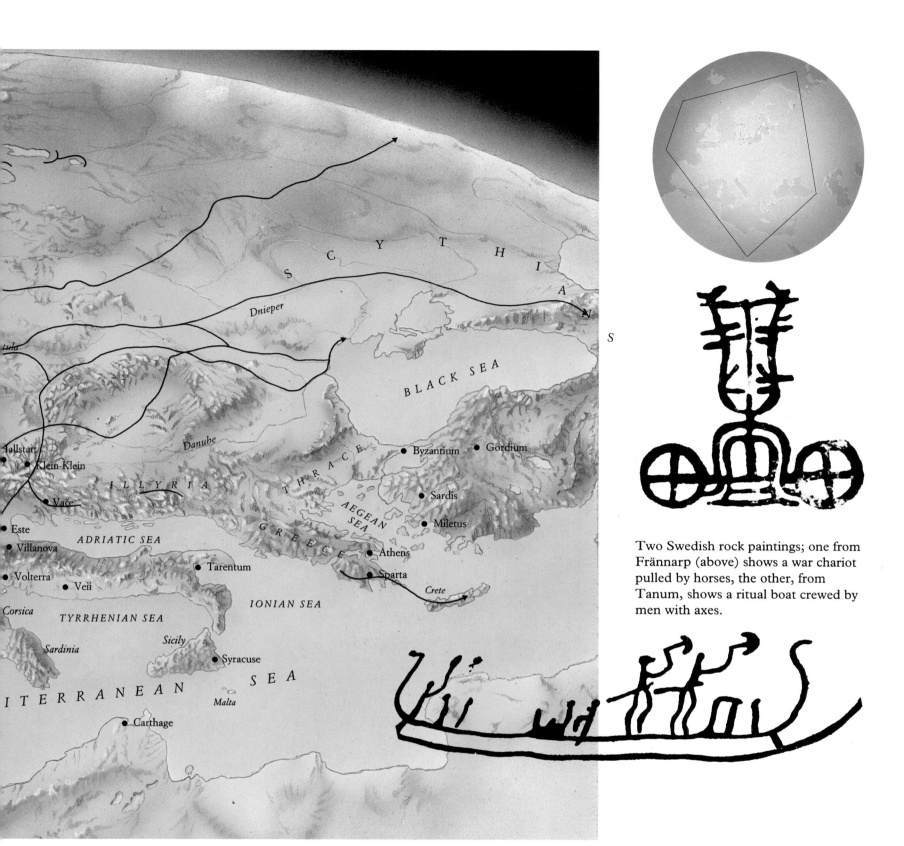

Two Swedish rock paintings; one from Frännarp (above) shows a war chariot pulled by horses, the other, from Tanum, shows a ritual boat crewed by men with axes.

6 NORDIC EUROPE IN THE BRONZE AGE

Around 1500 BC, knowledge of bronze-making reached the area south of Denmark, and thereafter spread north to Scandinavia. None of these lands had local sources of either copper or tin, and therefore no tradition of metal-working. Surprisingly, the quality of their workmanship was not inferior to that of other places in Europe where metal-working was established.

New technology through trade

The Scandinavian bronzeworkers evidently acquired the new technology through trade contacts with their southern neighbours. Trade was vigorous, thanks to efficient transport by sturdy boats suitable for river navigation, by large four-wheeled wagons that crossed flat plains without too much difficulty, and by the use of pack-horses able to cross mountains.

Around 1500 BC the first shiny bronze objects appeared in Denmark, probably imported from the British Isles. The Danish flint-crafters were stimulated to produce incredibly precise copies of bronze axes and knives, in stone. They even made stone swords, but though impeccably made, such weapons were fragile when compared with the new metal ones.

Later the Scandinavians learned to work bronze themselves, and bronze objects were made in Denmark. These were simple flat axes and knives, similar to those made by peoples of the Unětice culture of central Europe. In time, however, the Scandinavian metalworkers became masters of their own bronze styles, as shown by fish hooks, swords, battle-axes and spearheads found in Valsomagle in Zeeland. In spite of the Achaean-style double-spiral decoration, these tools are undoubtedly Scandinavian in origin.

How did they come by the design? There were trade contacts between Scandinavia and the Aegean, but these would have been via the trans-European trade in amber collected near the mouth of the River Elbe and in Jutland.

A Greek connection?

A less likely, but fascinating, theory is that Denmark got its name from the Danae, the Achaean people of Argolis in the Aegean. Mycenaean influence can be seen in rock engravings, for example, of war chariots on the stone tomb of Kivik in southern Sweden, and on rocks of Frännarp, Simris, Bohuslän and other sites in southern Norway. Similar chariots are shown engraved on funerary pillars at the port of Leoni near Mycenae, and in the second millennium BC these vehicles were widespread throughout the Mycenaean world.

We know quite a lot about the objects of Bronze Age Scandinavia, but very little about the people who made them. The picture (in colour on pages 24/25) is based on speculation and on the more detailed knowledge we have about later Scandinavia, when Celtic and Roman influences were present.

The people had boats. Pictures of their craft are found on rocks (as shown in the left-hand corner of the picture). For Scandinavians, their landscape of lakes, rivers and fjord-broken coastline made water transport essential.

The crew of this hide-covered rowing boat are warriors as well as sailors – like the Vikings who came many centuries later. The ox skull on the prow is a charm, against ill fortune. The warriors have bronze swords and shields, and their leader wears a horned helmet. In the background (left) is a ceremonial centre of standing stones. To the right is a fortified village. Two horsemen patrol the river bank. For these people, the rivers offered safer trade routes than the deep fjords and open sea.

This painting of human figures (opposite page) dancing in ritual costumes (perhaps of birds' feathers) comes from Sweden.

These rock paintings from Sweden (below) show riders on horses, with harnesses.

Tomb treasure and bronze horns

The Early Scandinavian Bronze Age (1500-900 BC) is characterized by huge tombs, almost 3 metres (9ft) high and 18 metres (59ft) across. These tombs were made from stones covered with turf, and placed either on hilltops, overlooking the surrounding land, or in rows one in front of the other, forming a kind of pathway.

The most elaborate tombs are in Egtved, Skrydstrup and Muldbjerg (all in Jutland). Here people were buried with articles they would need in the afterlife – leather goods, gold necklaces, wooden and horn items, boxes made of tree bark, animal skins, food and drink (beer and cider).

The most remarkable find of Nordic prehistory is the Trundholm 'sun chariot'. From this site in northwest Zeeland, archaeologists found a huge gold-plated disc, decorated in a series of circles and spirals, supported by six wheels and drawn by a bronze horse, shown in relief. The meaning of this object is unknown, but it is almost certainly connected with a sun cult, widely followed at this time.

The Late Scandinavian Bronze Age (900-400 BC) shows detailed decoration of weapons and ornamental objects. Tombs, like those in Kivik, contained stone burial chambers, engraved with human figures, chariots and mysterious drawings. People now began to cremate their dead, and this practice became common during the later Bronze Age in Scandinavia.

The most surprising finds from this last period (which corresponds to the middle Iron Age at Hallstatt) are *lurer*. The *lur* is a large, curving wind instrument, made of bronze (probably by the 'lost wax' method of moulding), and up to 2.5 metres (8ft) long. Pairs of these horns were probably played in religious rites. Also found are gold goblets, round bowls made from hammered bronze, horned helmets (probably belonging to famous warriors) and weapons copied from iron ones made by Hallstatt workers.

This razor (right), with a handle in the shape of a woman carrying a bowl, was found in Germany.

These two bronze figures of animals, probably deer, were found in Norway.

7 THE BRITISH ISLES

The map shows the settlement of the British Isles which took place over several periods. Before 3000 BC there were scattered groups of Old Stone Age hunters. New Stone Age hunters migrated occasionally to Britain from mainland Europe. From about 2500 BC there was fairly regular movement by sea, with animal herders arriving from the Mediterranean, by way of Iberia and France, and also from the Baltic lands. They are distinguished by their 'long-headed' (doliocephal) skulls and megalithic (stone slab) graves. About 2000 BC Bronze Age toolmakers arrived from Iberia and Germany. These 'round-skulled' Beaker people introduced a distinctive pottery. From about 800 BC iron-using peoples settled in southern Britain. Picts settled in the north. From about 600 BC Hallstatt culture is evident (from daggers and other objects). Celtic farmers cultivated small fields and dug pits to store grain.

This splendid ceremonial Celtic shield (pictured on the map) is made of bronze with red glass inset decoration. It was found in the River Thames in London.

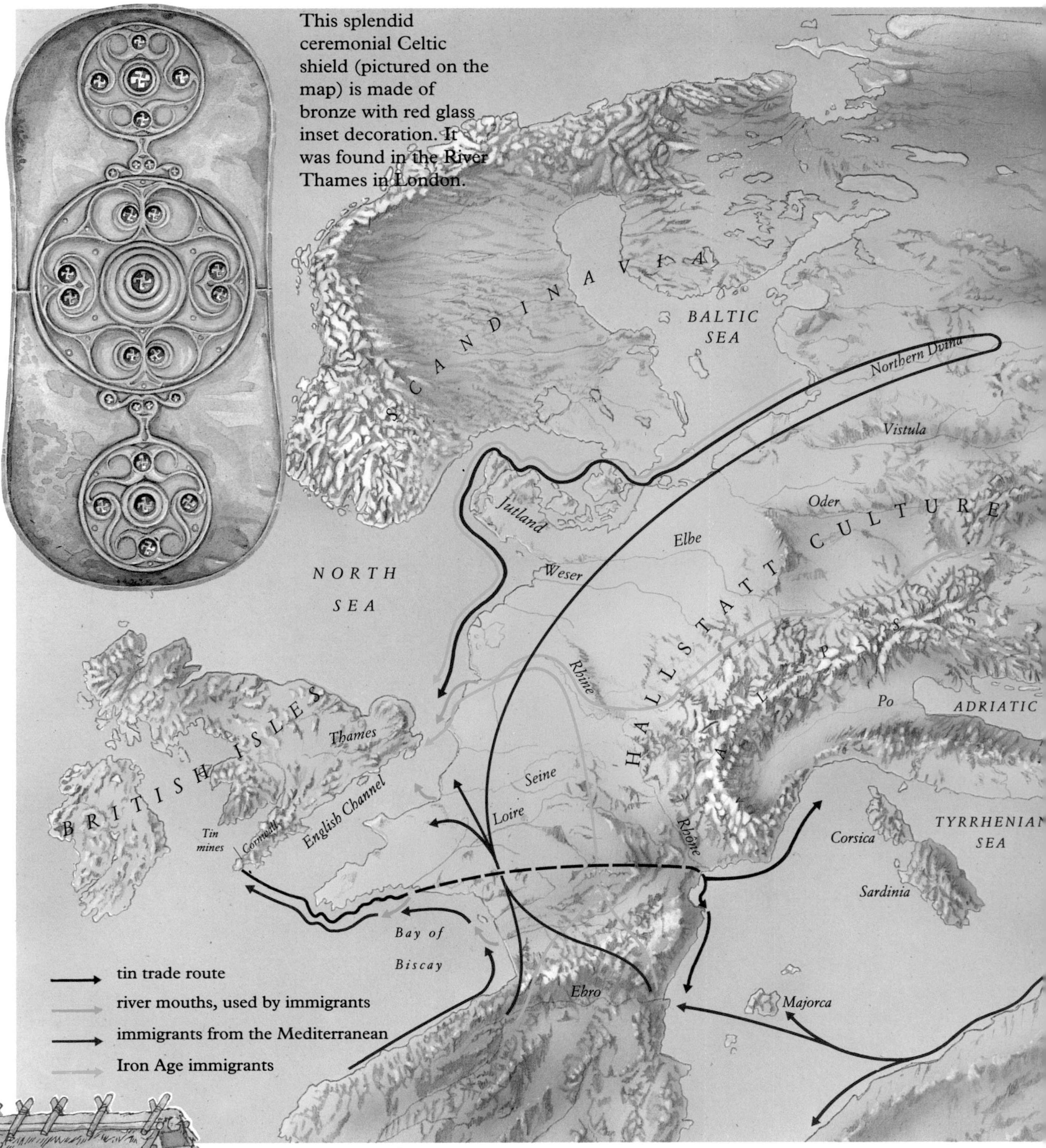

SCANDINAVIA

BALTIC SEA

Northern Dvina

Vistula

Jutland

Oder

Elbe

HALLSTATT CULTURE

Weser

NORTH SEA

Rhine

ALPS

Po

ADRIATIC

BRITISH ISLES

Thames

Seine

Corsica

TYRRHENIAN SEA

Loire

English Channel

Tin mines

Cornwall

Rhône

Sardinia

Bay of Biscay

Ebro

Majorca

- → tin trade route
- → river mouths, used by immigrants
- → immigrants from the Mediterranean
- → Iron Age immigrants

This magnificent gold-leaf necklace, or torque, probably belonged to a king or chieftain. It comes from Gleninsheen in Ireland and dates from the end of the Bronze Age.

Migrant departure areas
Bronze Age settlers
Iron Age settlers
▲ Neolithic sites
♦ Bronze Age sites
● Iron Age sites

BLACK SEA

Danube

ILLYRIA

THRACE

AEGEAN SEA

GREECE

SEA

IONIAN SEA

Sicily

Malta

ATLANTIC OCEAN

SCOTLAND

IRELAND

Isle of Man

Gleninsheen ♦

● Derrynablaha

Caergwrle ♦

WALES

ENGLAND

NORTH SEA

● Holderness

♦ Aust-on-Severn

▲ Avebury

Thames

▲ Stonehenge
● Salisbury

Exeter ▲

Cornwall

♦ Clandon Barrow

English Channel

Seine

The Neolithic period, or New Stone Age, started late in the British Isles and lasted until about 2000 BC. Around this time new migrants arrived, people with round skulls (unlike the longer-headed Stone Age people). They came from lands that we now know as the Netherlands and Germany, and they brought a distinctive pottery beaker which gives them their name: Beaker people.

Beakers and bronzes

Although bronze was new to Britain, Britain had helped to create the new technology. Bronze is an alloy of copper and tin, and Cornwall was Europe's richest source of tin. Tin was traded across the Channel, to make bronze.

The Beaker culture signalled the end of the New Stone Age in the British Isles. Bronze technology reached the islands from Spain, along the ancient trade routes following the coasts and rivers of western Europe. The southwest of England, from Cornwall to Salisbury Plain, was a rich region of megalithic culture. Stonehenge is the most famous example of stone monument building. The Beaker culture was widespread in the eastern part of Britain.

Builders of forts and farmers

The bronze-using Beaker people from northern Germany moved west to meet and mingle with the people of the stone-using culture. Across southern England, bronze-users built forts and earth ramparts to protect their farms. These people cremated their dead and then buried the ashes in urns.

The series of transformations in Britain at the end of the Neolithic period, and in the Bronze Age up to about 400 BC, were almost certainly due to successive influxes of peoples from Europe, who had adopted bronze- and then ironworking from the more advanced cultures of the Mediterranean.

Britain and Europe

During these centuries the British Isles went on absorbing influences from mainland Europe, much as they had earlier, when the islands were still physically joined to the continent. Culturally, the land was not an island, even if it was now separated from Europe by sea.

An important trade item was amber, and it seems that Britain was part of this trade, having links with Scandinavia and the Baltic. According to the Greek historian Herodotus, Britain acquired the bronze culture of Hallstatt, after a brief period of rule by Ligurians (a Mediterranean people), who were then driven out by Celts, using iron weapons. There are many theories as to whether change came through trade or conquest, in a time when the historical evidence is lacking.

This scene of southern England (pictured in colour on pages 28/29) shows a village at the time when Stone Age and Bronze Age cultures were merging. The people's lives were being changed, slowly, by progress in mainland Europe.

The villagers share the rearing of their animals, which are protected at night inside the fence. Cattle provide milk and meat, but the people are most proud of their horses, which are small but strong and fast. They ride, hunt and fight on horseback.

In the distance (right) is a hilltop fort-village, enclosed by a strong palisade. The villagers will take refuge inside the fort if enemies attack. The woman (left) is making stone tools, as people have done for thousands of years. Other tasks, such as grinding grain between stones, are also unchanged since Stone Age times. But the men working by the fire are using a new technology; they are trying to shape a piece of bronze into a sword.

The village huts are made of stone, with sloping roofs covered in thatch of straw or reeds. Life offers few luxuries – a wild duck brought in by the boy hunter will make a tasty addition to the people's diet.

This stylized wooden ship (right) comes from Yorkshire. It is shaped like a snake and its four armed warriors have moving limbs. Their eyes are made of quartz.

Found in southern Britain, this figure (below) was made from Spanish bronze, and illustrates how continental influences reached Britain.

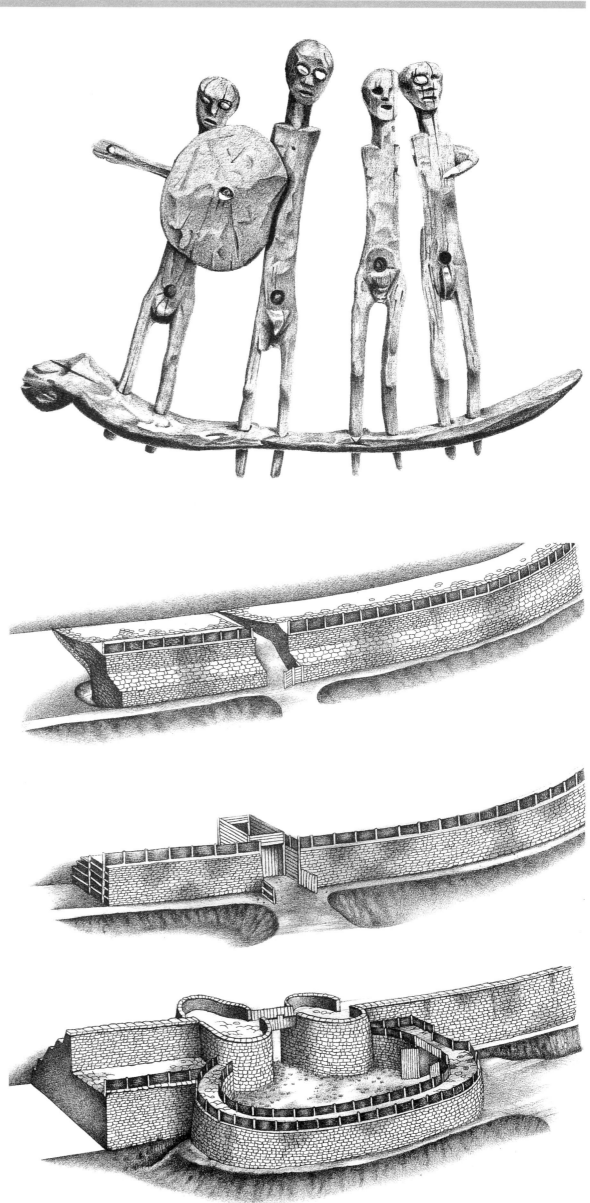

These pictures (right) show three stages in the development of a fortified camp, uncovered at Crickley Hill in Gloucestershire. The Neolithic camp (top) has earth and stone walls. The gateway defences were strengthened in the Iron Age fort (centre), when the walls were made of stones locked in place by timbers. Later the gateway was made even more impregnable, by the addition of towers and an outer wall.

8 THE IBERIANS

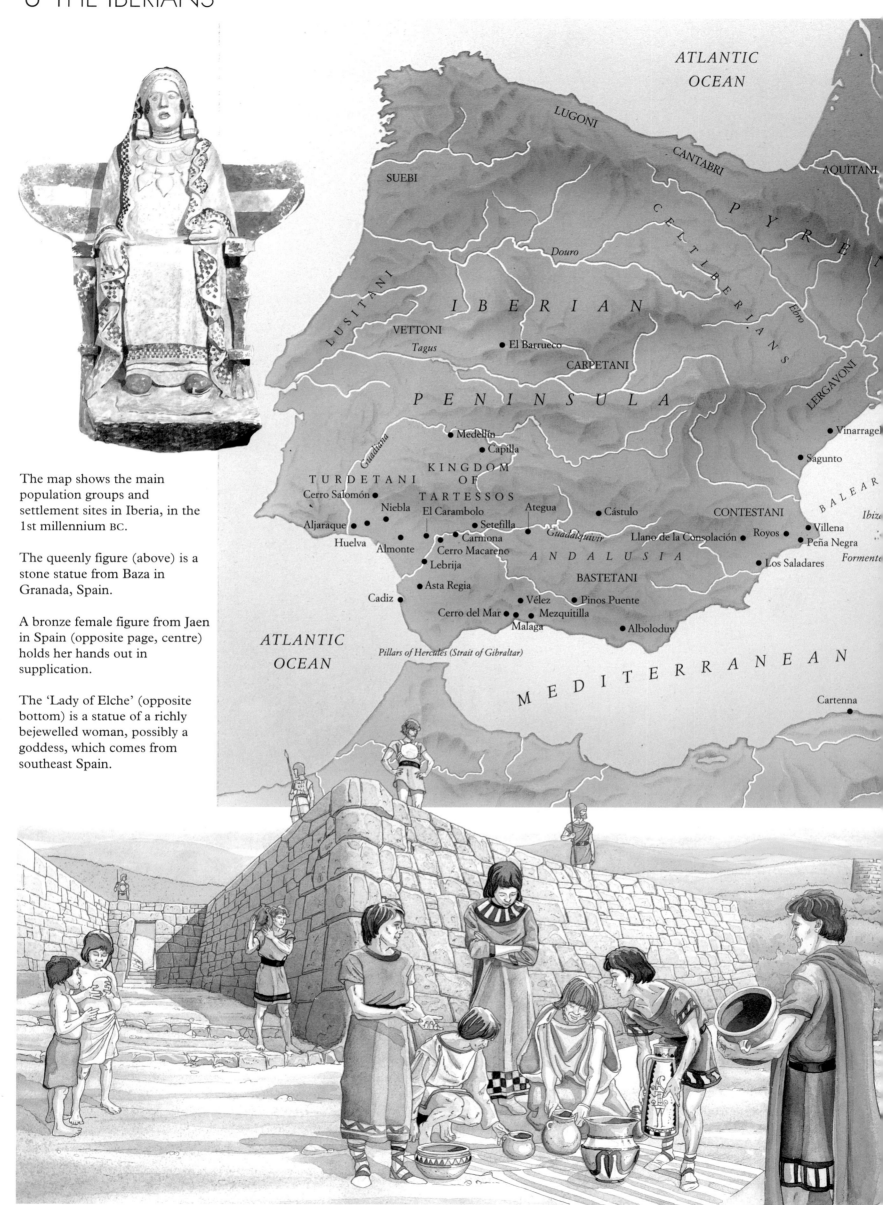

ATLANTIC
OCEAN

LUGONI

CANTABRI

AQUITANI

SUEBI

LUSITANI

VETTONI

Douro

CELTIBERIANS

Ebro

PYRE

I B E R I A N

El Barrueco

CARPETANI

LERGAVONI

P E N I N S U L A

Guadiana

Medellín

Capilla

Vinarrage

Sagunto

KINGDOM
OF

TURDETANI

Cerro Salomón

T A R T E S S O S

BALEAR

Ibiza

Niebla

El Carambolo

Ategua

Cástulo

CONTESTANI

Aljaraque

Setefilla

Carmona

Guadalquivir

Llano de la Consolación

Royos

Villena

Huelva

Almonte

Cerro Macareno

A N D A L U S I A

Peña Negra

Formente

Lebrija

Los Saladares

Asta Regia

BASTETANI

Cadiz

Vélez

Pinos Puente

Cerro del Mar

Mezquitilla

Malaga

Alboloduy

Pillars of Hercules (Strait of Gibraltar)

ATLANTIC
OCEAN

M E D I T E R R A N E A N

Cartenna

The map shows the main
population groups and
settlement sites in Iberia, in the
1st millennium BC.

The queenly figure (above) is a
stone statue from Baza in
Granada, Spain.

A bronze female figure from Jaen
in Spain (opposite page, centre)
holds her hands out in
supplication.

The 'Lady of Elche' (opposite
bottom) is a statue of a richly
bejewelled woman, possibly a
goddess, which comes from
southeast Spain.

L. Geneva

L. Maggiore

L. Como

L. Garda

ALPS

Rhône

Po

Ticino

Adda

Adige

Po

Arno

Loire

Garonne

ERRETANI

ES

Massilia

LIGURIAN SEA

Ullastret

Emporiae

Elba

Corsica

Alalia

Tiber

ISLANDS

Minorca

Majorca

Sardinia

Tharros

TYRRHENIAN
SEA

Sulchis

Cagliari

SEA

Rusucurra

Hippo (Bizerta)

Sicily

Motya

Hippo (Bône)

Utica

Carthage

8 THE IBERIANS

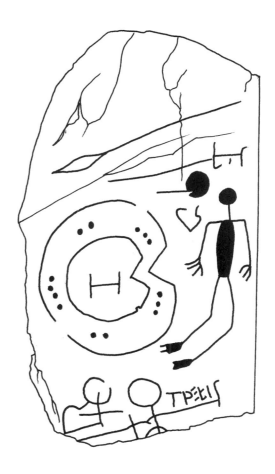

Towards the end of the Bronze Age, the peoples of the Iberian Peninsula (Spain and Portugal) began to settle along the coasts, leaving the inland settlements that they had inhabited for centuries. The move brought them into contact with new cultures. The coastal regions (which included the valley of the Guadalquivir river in Andalusia) were more suited to crop-growing and animal-rearing, and people settling there could control the trade routes to the mines inland. Minerals were an important Iberian trade product. The Iberians built simple hill villages, defended by walls.

The Phoenicians in Spain

The Phoenicians, who had traded with Iberia for some time without settling permanently, founded a colony at Cadiz on the southwest coast. Attempts to settle along the Atlantic coast at Huelva failed because of opposition from local people. The Phoenicians had to content themselves with trade colonies on the east coast, between Malaga and Catalonia. But during the first half of the 8th century BC, Cadiz and the region surrounding it was already the key area for further western colonization.

Cadiz was vital because it gave the Phoenicians control of the Strait of Gibraltar, and access for trade to the kingdom of Tartessos (called Tarshish in the Bible). This was the most important Spanish kingdom. Its exact location is disputed, but was probably in eastern Andalusia between Huelva and the shallow course of the Guadalquivir river. According to legend, it was ruled by cruel kings, including the three-headed monster Geryon, from whom Hercules stole cattle after he placed the rock of Gibraltar at the end of the world.

Mineral wealth and Tartessos

Huelva was one of the richest mining regions in the Mediterranean. From its mines came copper and silver. The Tartessians also traded in tin, which they combined with copper to make bronze. It was for good reason that the Greeks called Huelva 'the golden-appled garden of the Hesperides'. The Guadalquivir river was a route inland to the mines.

The Tartessian culture reached its peak around 700-600 BC. The wealth of Tartessos also attracted the Greeks, who competed with the Phoenicians for trade and colonies. The kings of Tartessos seem to have been friendly with the

The picture (shown in colour in pages 32/33) is a reconstruction of the walls of Tartessos in the 500s BC. The walls are in Greek fortress style, built of stone. Watch-towers guard the coast against pirates and trade rivals.

Tartessos was a rich kingdom, thanks to its trade in metals and luxury goods brought by the Greek and Phoenician ships. Two Phoenician ships are beached in the bay below the town. Ships arrive almost every day, from trade bases along the Atlantic coast of Spain, such as Cadiz.

People inspect the newly arrived foods eagerly. The Phoenician merchants offer pottery, bronze vessels, dyed cloth and heavy Eastern-style jewellery. In exchange, they will take gold, silver and copper from the mines inland. Spain's precious metals were

shipped east through the Mediterranean, protected by the Phoenician navy. Warriors with bronze weapons and armour stand guard over this powerful kingdom, which was to disappear from history and of which as yet we know tantalizingly little.

The procession of dancers (above) appears as a decoration on a piece of pottery from Lliria, Spain.

This fragment of a tomb (opposite page) comes from Solana de Cabañas, Caseres, Spain. It is engraved with a picture of the dead man and his weapons. Above the large shield are his spear and sword, and below is a war chariot.

These bronze figures (right) show an armed warrior (left) and another man offering a pomegranate. They come from El Collado de los Jardines, Jaen, Spain.

This picture (bottom) comes from a piece of pottery, and shows a man breaking (taming) a horse, and three dogs. Horses were highly valued by the Iberians, who used them for hunting and war, and sold them abroad.

Greeks and with the Phocians. The most famous of these rulers was King Arganthonios, for whom Greek settlers built a city wall.

The importance of ports

Greeks and Phoenicians were both settling in Spain at the same time. Their cultures were absorbed by the Tartessians and influenced other peoples inland. The Phocians (Greeks from Phocis in central Greece) founded a colony at Emporiae on the shores of the western Mediterranean. This was well sited to support Massilia (Marseilles), a port which had grown in importance with the trade in tin and other goods from the north coming through the Rhône river valley.

In the 400s BC Emporiae was a key port for coastal trade with Andalusia. Sagunto became another important market and port town. The Phoenicians controlled the silver mines around Villaricos, and guarded the sea routes to the island of Ibiza, a port of call for ships voyaging between Cadiz, Carthage and the East, stopping en route at Tharros (Sardinia) and Motya (Sicily). Later the Phoenician colonies were taken over by Carthage.

9 Peoples of Italy and the Tyrrhenian Islands

This fantastical bronze warrior (right) has four eyes, four arms and two shields. He is probably a god, and was found at Abini in Sardinia.

The plan (below) shows several Sardinian *nuraghi*, or round towers, developed over centuries into a castle complex. The central tower (grey) was possibly the first; coloured areas indicate later additions – green, yellow, red, and finally white (in Punic-Roman times).

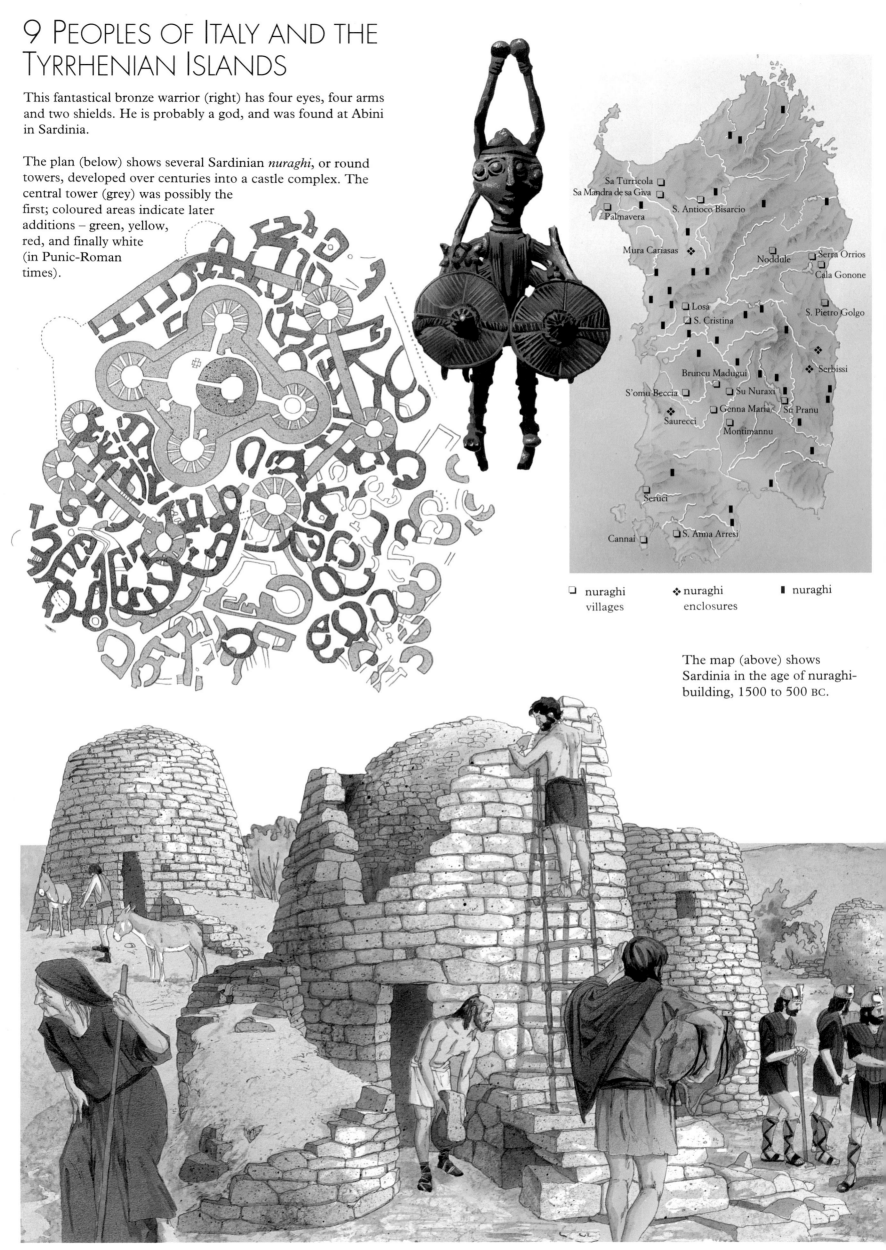

The map (above) shows Sardinia in the age of nuraghi-building, 1500 to 500 BC.

☐ nuraghi villages   ❖ nuraghi enclosures   ▪ nuraghi

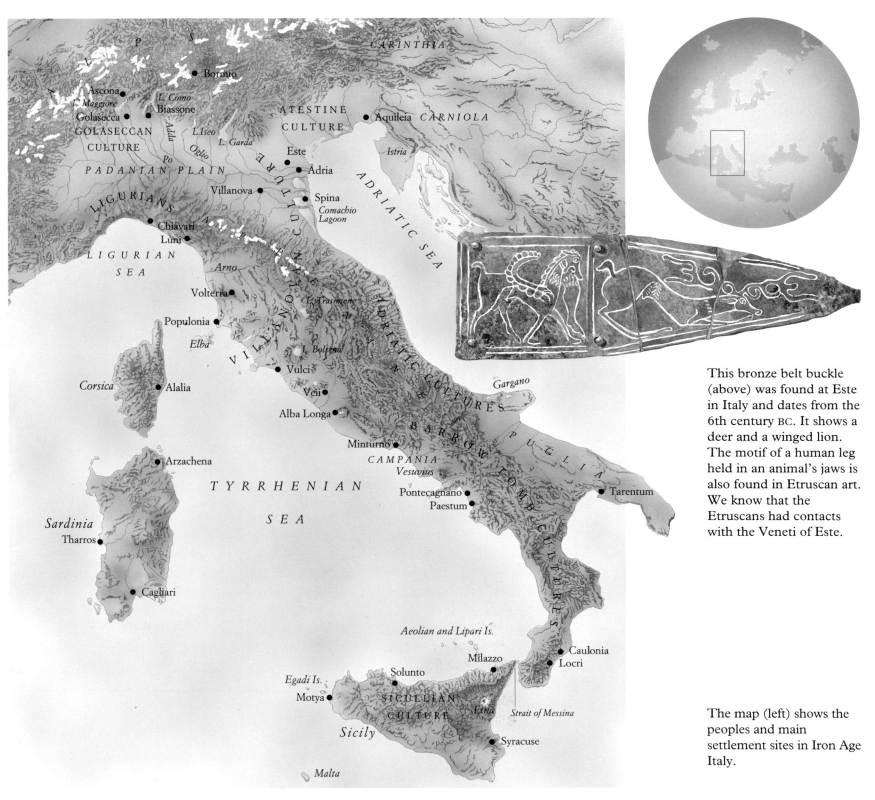

This bronze belt buckle (above) was found at Este in Italy and dates from the 6th century BC. It shows a deer and a winged lion. The motif of a human leg held in an animal's jaws is also found in Etruscan art. We know that the Etruscans had contacts with the Veneti of Este.

The map (left) shows the peoples and main settlement sites in Iron Age Italy.

9 PEOPLES OF ITALY AND THE TYRRHENIAN ISLANDS

A large vase made by the Daunic people of Apulia, southern Italy. It is decorated with a lively animal head and a geometric pattern. It was probably used for water.

Before the 1st century BC, by which time the Romans had united Italy by conquest, the country was inhabited by a mix of peoples with different languages, cultures, religions and social systems. Some had lived in the region since the Stone Age, others were immigrants from other parts of Europe. Some stayed in one location for a long time, others wandered about the country as nomads before settling.

A medley of languages

The first peoples of Italy are difficult to identify clearly. They probably spoke non-Indo-European languages, and perhaps were related to people living in the Aegean and Asia Minor regions. People from the Alps and the Adriatic, who spoke Indo-European languages, arrived during the 2000s BC, and occupied a large part of Italy.

Some groups, such as the Latins, Umbrians, Siculians, Greeks and Celts, spoke Indo-European languages. Others like the Ligurians, Sicanians and northern Picenians spoke other languages, unrelated to the Indo-European family of languages.

Contacts and influences

The two main influences on these peoples were perhaps the superior eastern Mycenaean culture (until it collapsed in the 10th century BC) and the Urnfield culture of north-central Europe (see page 22). By the 700s BC peoples with their own languages, customs and societies had emerged – notably the Etruscans, Latins, Venetians and Ligurians.

In the 800s new cultural contacts had been made with Greece and the East, as Greeks and Phoenicians founded colonies in southern Italy, Sicily and Sardinia. The Greek influence grew stronger all the time, and was of great advantage to Etruria, which during the Iron Age developed a vigorous culture of its own.

In the south, Brutians and Lucanians moved into territory occupied by less developed peoples, pushing the Siculians across the Strait of Messina into Sicily. Sicanians in Sicily were driven westwards. Other peoples on the move were the Samnites in the southern Apennine region, the Umbrians who settled along the river Tiber, and the Latins.

The Etruscan homeland

The area between the rivers Tiber and Arno (most of north-central Italy) was Etruscan. Westward were the

The scene (shown in colour on pages 36/37) shows people in Sardinia building an addition to their defensive complex of nuraghi – round forts made of basalt, a volcanic rock.

These people were known as Sards. They lived in settlements and were devoted to cereal cultivation and animal-rearing. To protect themselves and their farms from attack, the Sards built their villages on a fortress pattern. They began by building a central tower like the keep of a medieval castle. This was developed by adding other stages.

The walls of each tower were made from stone blocks cemented together with mud. The interior space was divided into circular rooms, for people and animals, for donkeys, sheep and goats shared the fort with their owners. Narrow passageways wound between the walls (as shown in the plan on page 36).

Every day the villagers left their fort to till their fields or to herd their sheep and goats on the hill pastures, where they built other small forts for defence against raiders.

This tombstone of a Ligurian warrior, shown holding iron weapons, was found in Tuscany.

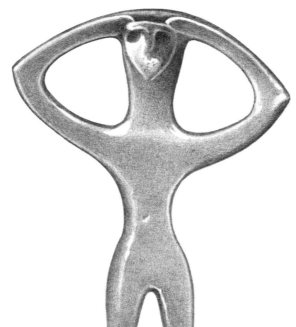

This clay figurine was made in the 6th century BC, and comes from Teramo in Italy.

A parting scene is shown on this fragment of a Daunic funeral stone. The people bidding farewell have stylized 'bird' faces. The man carries a pack on a pole, as a traveller would. The woman (right) carries a pot on her head.

Ligurians, who lived in a region bordering the Alps and the River Rhône. Another mountain people living north of the River Po were the Rhaetians, to the southeast of whom lived the Veneti. On the islands of Sardinia and Corsica in the Tyrrhenian Sea lived peoples who, it is thought, were descended from ancient Iberian peoples.

Added to these peoples were other groups such as the Daunic people, who originated in the Balkans and settled in southern Italy. Each had its own territory, and together they made up the population of the peninsula we now call Italy. The concept of a land united under one ruler came later, with the Romans. Indeed the islands of Sicily, Sardinia and Corsica, which is now part of France, were not considered or governed as part of Italy at all until the 3rd century AD.

The Warrior of Capestrano is a part-painted limestone statue from a tomb of a Sabellian leader. On the warrior's head is a broad-brimmed helmet or hat, and he is wearing a mask. This 6th-century BC sculpture is considered one of the most important pre-Roman discoveries in central Italy.

This cheese-making utensil, used as a strainer and funnel, was found in a burial site at Campovalano and dates from the 6th century BC.

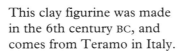

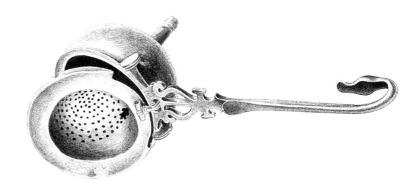

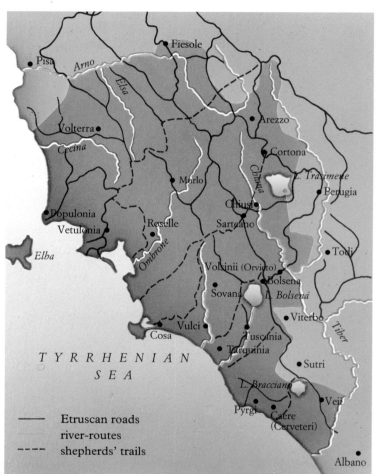

The map (above) shows north-central Italy about 900-800 BC, with areas of Villanovan influence in green.

This vase (left) is possibly by a Greek artist. The black-painted figures show the giant Polyphemus being blinded. The vase came from Cerveteri, and was made about 530 BC.

Etruscan roads
river-routes
shepherds' trails

These cutaway pictures show a burial mound. The tombs are deep underground and covered with a tumulus, on which vegetation has grown (left). They are reached via a passage. The ashes of a person of high rank are contained in an urn inside the brick chamber (above), along with other grave goods.

L. Maggiore
L. Como
L. Iseo
L. Garda

V E N E T I

Mantua
Adige
Adria
Po
Spina
Bologna
Ravenna
Chiavari
Rimini
Luni

L I G U R I A N
S E A

Pisa
Arno
Fiesole
Volterra
Arezzo
Cortona
Numana

A D R I A T I C   S E A

P I C E N I A N S

Populonia
L. Trasimene
Perugia
Roselle
Chiusi
Elba
Vetulonia
Talamone
Bolsena
L. Bolsena
Vulci
Tiber
Corsica
Tarquinia
Ferentino
Alalia
Caere
(Cerveteri)
Veii

S A M N I T E S

L A T I N I

Satrico

Arzachena
Minturno
Canosa
Capua
Ofanto

C A M P A N I A

Cumae

T Y R R H E N I A N
S E A

Sardinia
Grumento

The map (opposite page, right) shows Etruria, with its main trade and military routes. The shepherds' trails were used to take sheep to seasonal pastures.

The map (above) shows the greatest extent of the Etruscans' power (in red), before they were overcome by Rome (200s BC).

The Etruscan helmet (left) acted as the lid of a funerary urn.

10 THE ETRUSCANS

In the 9th century BC, a culture developed in north-central Italy which united peoples of Indo-European language stock. This culture has been named Villanovan, after the site of Villanova near Bologna where the first of their distinctive cemeteries was found in 1853.

The Villanovans

The Villanovans were skilled metalworkers. They cremated their dead, and then buried the ashes in two-part conical urns. With the ashes they buried personal items such as brooches, rings, ear-rings, spearheads and votive statues. Cremation was also common elsewhere in northern Italy, in Lombardy, the Veneto and the Alpine districts.

Around the middle of the 8th century BC, the Etruscans first appeared around the river Po and the Tyrrhenian coastal region which was Villanovan territory. Their funeral customs were different; they buried their dead. The Etruscans developed a new culture which came to dominate the north of Italy.

The mysterious Etruscans

Where the Etruscans came from is much discussed. Many experts think that they were the descendants of older peoples of Italy. Others claim that they came by sea from the Middle East, and in particular from Lydia (a region of western Anatolia, now Turkey). Similarities in their alphabets support this idea. Another less likely theory suggests that the Etruscans came from the north, as invaders across the Alps, during the Indo-European migrations that began in the 2nd millennium BC.

More scholars now believe, however, that the Villanovans were the ancestors of the Etruscans, despite the differences

in their funeral customs. What is clear is that the Etruscans were remarkably successful in dominating other peoples. They had contacts with all the important Mediterranean cultures, and their territory was rich in natural resources such as cereals, olive oil, wine, iron and copper.

Etruscan city-states

At first Etruria was a land of city-states on the model of the Greek *polis*. These states were united by one language and a common origin, but their customs differed (some still cremated their dead, like the Villanovans). The varied geography of their lands also influenced the development of different economies.

The aim of these cities was to control metal production, and secure trade routes by land and sea. To these ends, the

A fortified city in Etruria (shown in colour on pages 40/41). The Etruscan heartland was defended by walled cities, such as Veii (Veio), Caere (Cerveteri), Tarquinia and Volsinii (Orvieto).

Fortified cities were built on high ground, to guard a trade route, or a route used by sheep during seasonal drives to fresh pasture. From the walls of this town the soldiers keep watch on the fields below, and can view the coast. They can communicate with their neighbours in another walled town (right of picture). Cities were built in places vital to travel – rivers, lakes and valley mouths – to protect the Etruscans' food supply and their trade in farm produce and metals. Examples of such guard-cities (shown on the map on page 40) include Perugia, in the Tiber Valley, near Lake Trasimene; and Roselle on the lagoon of Prilio which controlled the mouth of the river Ombrone, one of the few rivers giving access to the interior of Etruria.

Inside the city walls are well-built houses and an atmosphere of business-like orderliness. Many people enjoy a fairly comfortable standard of living. Ox-carts and donkeys transport the goods on which Etruscan prosperity depended.

The coast was much less populated. The port of Populonia was one settlement, close to the iron mines on the island of Elba (see maps).

One of the most famous examples of Etruscan art (opposite page), this statue of a couple on a couch was made in the late 6th century BC and found at Cerveteri. It is actually a funeral urn, made to contain the ashes of the dead pair, and was originally painted.

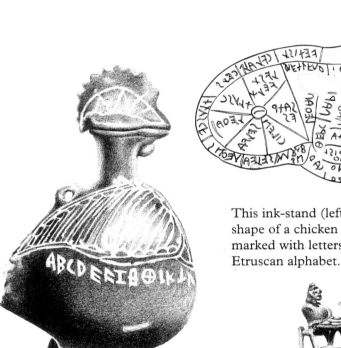

This bronze model of a sheep's liver (top right) dates from the 3rd century BC, and was found near Piacenza. It was used by Etruscan augurers (fortune-tellers) to teach pupils their art. The liver was thought to reflect the universe, and was sectioned into 40 areas corresponding to divinities. The augurers tried to predict, from examination of the livers of sacrificed animals, how many gods were present and what people might expect or fear from them. The line drawing below the picture shows the writing more clearly; it is in the Greek-style Etruscan alphabet.

cities were linked by religious and military alliances. They collaborated in trade, extending their commerce north to the Po Valley and across the Alps. To the south, they secured the economic dependence of the Latins. The Etruscans reclaimed marshland by draining it and by digging canals, to improve their agriculture. They placed great value on good communications, from which each city drew economic benefit and political prestige.

The Etruscan league

The Etruscans formed a league of 12 cities into a kind of federation. Cities may have belonged only intermittently to this important grouping, as the power of each one rose and fell. Originally each city had its own king, but he was replaced in time (as happened in Greece) by a group of noble families. The names of these families, such as the Matuna of Cerveteri and the Pumpu of Tarquinia, and the tombs set aside for their members, are known. Many bore the title *maru*, and held the office of priest; others were called *puth*, meaning tyrant.

Beneath the ruling, landowning aristocracy was a well-to-do middle class, of people who had made their fortune by trade and commerce. They demanded a share in public life, but never managed to unseat the aristocracy. The lower classes (farm labourers, artisans, slaves – and foreigners) remained subservient.

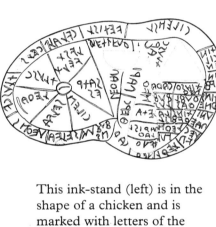

This ink-stand (left) is in the shape of a chicken and is marked with letters of the Etruscan alphabet.

A 7th-century BC funerary urn from Montescudaio, Volterra, Italy. It is Villanovan in shape, but has Etruscan decoration. On the handle is a bearded male figure; on the lid the same figure sits at a funeral feast.

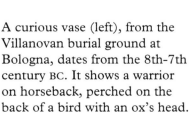

A curious vase (left), from the Villanovan burial ground at Bologna, dates from the 8th-7th century BC. It shows a warrior on horseback, perched on the back of a bird with an ox's head.

11 MEDITERRANEAN VOYAGERS

The map shows the main ports and shipping routes of the Greeks (Ionians and Dorians), Phoenicians and Etruscans.

The terracotta mask (below), with its grotesque hand-shaped features, dates from the 7th-6th centuries BC.

The blue pendant (opposite page) is made from coloured glass, and was hung about the neck. It is Phoenician and comes from Olbia, Sardinia.

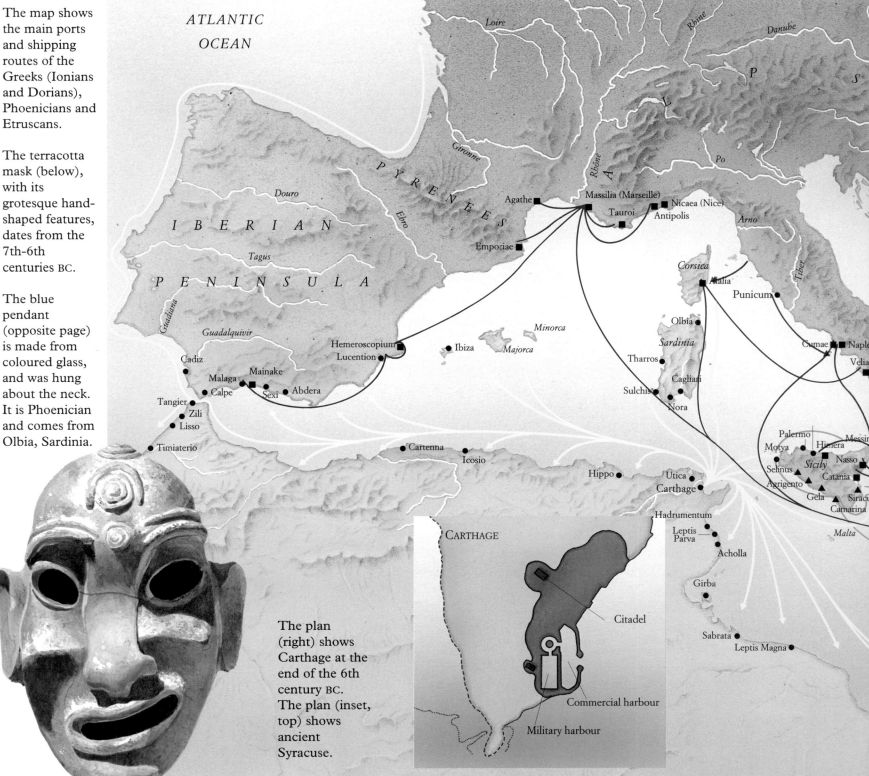

ATLANTIC OCEAN

IBERIAN PENINSULA

Douro

Tagus

Guadiana

Guadalquivir

Ebro

PYRENEES

Gironne

Loire

Rhône

Rhine

Danube

ALPS

Po

Arno

Tiber

Agathe

Massilia (Marseille)

Tauroi

Antipolis

Nicaea (Nice)

Emporiae

Corsica

Alalia

Punicum

Cadiz

Malaga

Calpe

Sexi

Abdera

Tangier

Zili

Lisso

Timiaterio

Mainake

Hemeroscopium

Lucention

Ibiza

Majorca

Minorca

Olbia

Sardinia

Tharros

Cagliari

Sulchis

Nora

Cumae

Naples

Velia

Cartenna

Icosio

Hippo

Utica

Carthage

Palermo

Motya

Selinus

Agrigento

Himera

Sicily

Gela

Messir

Nasso

Catania

Siracu

Camarina

Malta

Hadrumentum

Leptis Parva

Acholla

Girba

Sabrata

Leptis Magna

CARTHAGE

Citadel

Commercial harbour

Military harbour

The plan (right) shows Carthage at the end of the 6th century BC. The plan (inset, top) shows ancient Syracuse.

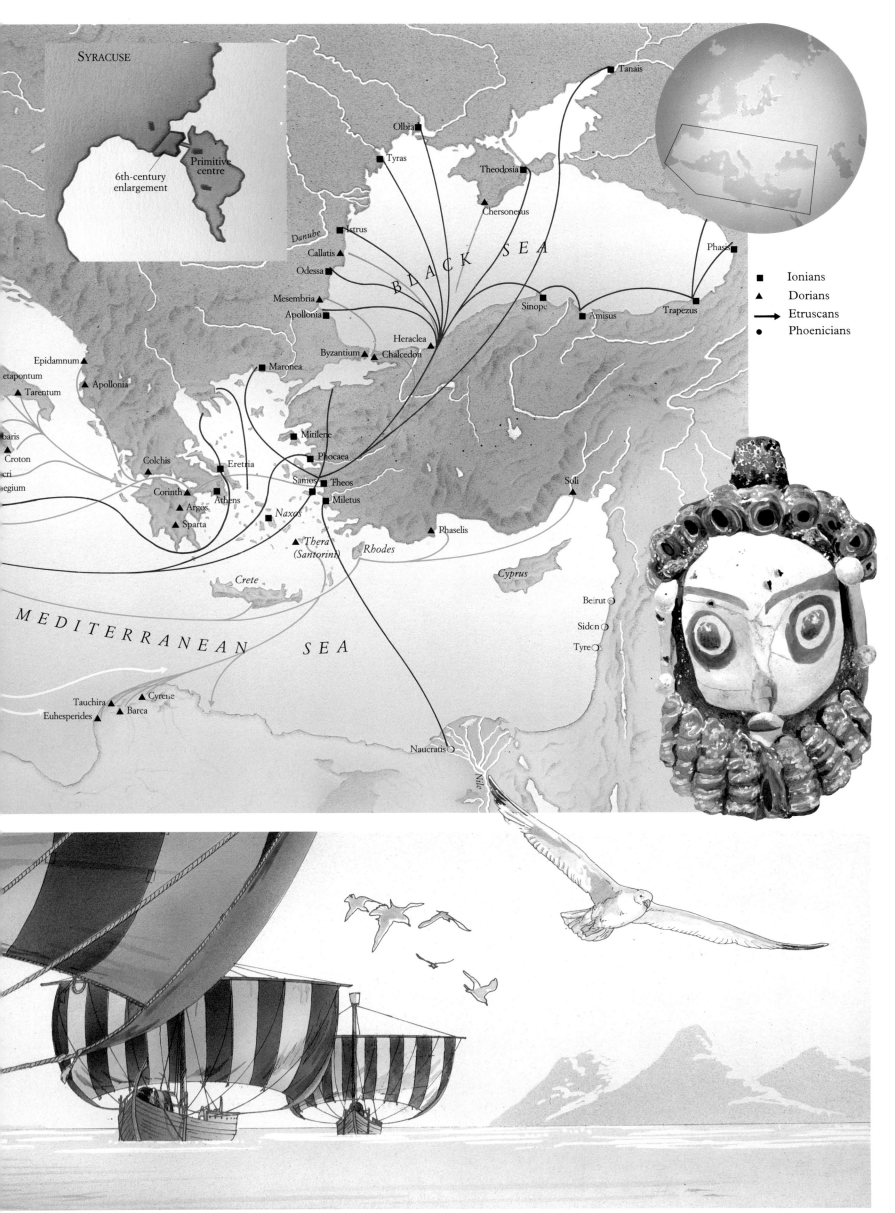

SYRACUSE

6th-century
enlargement

Primitive
centre

Tanais ■

Olbia ■

Tyras ■

Theodosia ■

Chersonesus ▲

Danube

Istrus ■

Callatis ▲

Odessa ■

Phasis ■

BLACK SEA

Mesembria ▲

Apollonia ■

Sinope ■

Amisus ■

Trapezus ■

Heraclea ▲

Byzantium ▲ ▲ Chalcedon

Epidamnum ▲

etapontum

▲ Apollonia

▲ Tarentum

Maronea ■

baris

Croton

cri

egium

Colchis ▲

Eretria ■

Mitilene ■

Phocaea ■

Soli ▲

Corinth ▲ ■ Athens
Samos ■ ■ Theos

Argos ▲
▲ Sparta

■ Miletus

Naxos ■

*Thera
(Santorini)* ▲

Rhodes

Phaselis ▲

Crete

Cyprus

Beirut ○

M E D I T E R R A N E A N   S E A

Sidon ○

Tyre ○

Tauchira ▲ ▲ Cyrene

Euhesperides ▲ ▲ Barca

Naucratis ○

Nile

■ Ionians

▲ Dorians

→ Etruscans

● Phoenicians

45

11 MEDITERRANEAN VOYAGERS

A terracotta goat (right), from Lebanon, the Phoenician homeland.

This painted pitcher (below) is also from Lebanon.

Carthage, on the shores of North Africa, was founded in 814 BC, according to tradition, by the Phoenicians of Tyre (modern Lebanon). Its Phoenician name was Kart-Hadasht, meaning 'new city'. The nearby city of Utica was known as the 'old city', and according to the Roman historian Pliny was founded in 1101 BC.

The Phoenicians and Carthage

Phoenician colonies were founded with the aim of controlling the sea, not the inland region. The Phoenicians were a sea people, the most famous traders and navigators of the ancient Mediterranean. Since the sea was their main concern, it was many hundreds of years before Carthage grew beyond its original limits at the end of a narrow peninsula on the shore of the Gulf of Tunis. It was easily defended, with a safe anchorage and a citadel, the Byrsa, on a low hill overlooking the sea.

From Carthage, settlers moved to Ibiza in 654 BC and about 50 years later to the south coast of Spain. The Phoenicians came to control the sea routes to the Iberian Peninsula and those around Sicily, where they set up bases. Their dominance was challenged by the arrival of the Greeks, and the Phoenicians had to share Sicily with their rivals – establishing their settlements on the west coast of the island, where they could still control the sea trade to Carthage itself and the silver mines and cities of the North African coast.

The Greek colonizers

The Greeks began founding colonies in southern Italy and Sicily. Cumae, their first western colony, was established about 750 BC, and Greeks settled in Motya (Sicily) towards

This small bronze figure (opposite page, left) was found in the sea near Selinunte, Sicily.

This reconstruction of Carthage (opposite page, right) shows the protected naval base, with anchorage for 220 galleys and the trading port. Little remains of this once-mighty city.

the end of the 700s, sharing the land with the Siculian people who already lived there. Greek colonization was one of the largest population movements of the ancient Mediterranean world. It was more complex than the Phoenician colonization, and was motivated primarily by the Greek desire to rebuild trade after years of decline following the collapse of the Mycenaean civilization, as well as by the need to feed and supply the growing city-states of Greece.

Dorians and Ionians took part in this seaward move-

Phoenician ships on a trading voyage (pictured in colour on pages 44/45). They are sailing together, for protection against pirates and because this was probably usual practice for merchant ships – if one ship was damaged in a storm, the others could rescue its crew and precious cargo. The crews know their routes well, following coastal landmarks, and navigating by the stars.

The Phoenicians' rivals in the Mediterranean were two other trading peoples – the Greeks and Etruscans. The Etruscans controlled land routes in Italy.

The Greeks and Phoenicians were rivals at sea, as far west as Spain and the Rock of Gibraltar.

Mostly this rivalry was peaceful, but the two seagoing traders and colonizers contested key bases such as those in western Sicily. More damaging to trade was the threat from pirates, who were to be found among the seamen of all the seagoing peoples of the Mediterranean. Lipari and Corsica were bases for Greek pirates. These seamen keep a sharp lookout for unfriendly sails, as they head for their next port of call with cargoes of wine and dyed cloth, or silver and iron.

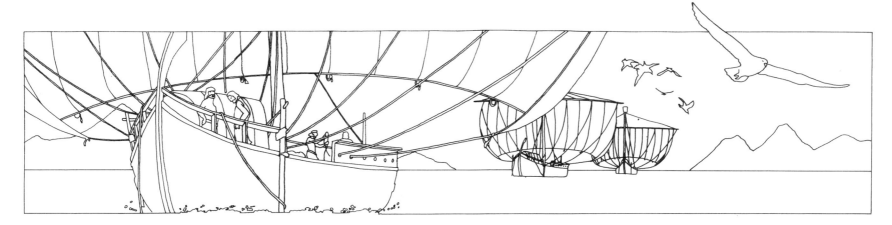

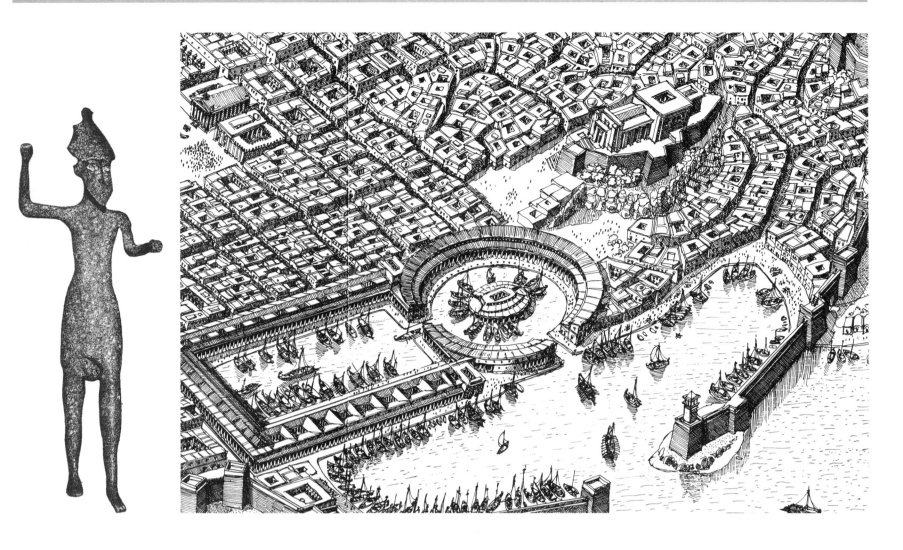

ment, coming from Rhodes, Crete, Corinth and Argos (Doric) and from Eretria, Naxos and Calchis (Ionian). Though they set up separate settlements, there was no great rivalry between them. Corinth became a key centre of this colonial activity, and kept a firm hold on its colonies. Other colonies, although under the patronage of mother-cities in Greece, were from the start independent, and linked to Greece only by ties of family, sentiment and religion. There was no Greek 'empire' in the west.

Relations between Phoenicians and Greeks

The Greeks and Phoenicians traded with one another, and exchanged cultural ideas. They do not seem to have clashed militarily before the 600s. Their interests were not the same; the Phoenicians wanted ports, anchorages and routes for their ships, and markets. The Greeks were more interested in land for settlement and farming. Not until the end of the 7th century BC do signs of tension between Sicilian Greeks and Phoenicians begin to show.

In 631 BC Greek settlers from Thera founded a colony called Cyrene on the African coast, to trade between Carthage and Egypt. Some years previously the Phocian Greeks had been successful in opening up the kingdom of Tartessos (Spain) to Greek trade. At the same time, in the late 600s BC, the Greeks began to show more interest in western Sicily. All these developments threatened the Phoenicians' interests.

The rise of Carthage

From 580 BC the Greeks attempted to push the Phoenicians out of Sicily, and Carthage intervened for the first

time. This was the beginning of the rise of Carthage as an empire. The Carthaginians enforced their control of Sicily, and then turned to Sardinia where they extended their rule beyond the ports and trading bases to the whole island.

The pirate threat

The Phocians, operating from a base at Alalia in Corsica, continued to be a problem. Phocian pirates raided in the Tyrrhenian Sea, annoying the Etruscans as well as the Phoenicians. In 540 BC the Etruscans and Carthaginians joined forces to destroy the Phocian pirates. Corsica became an Etruscan island, and the Phoenician/Carthaginian colonies in Sardinia were safe.

But now Etruscan power was on the decline. The Etruscans lost their influence over Rome, where in 509 BC the people drove out the last Etruscan king, Tarquinius Priscus (Tarquin the Proud). A naval defeat in 474 BC at Cumae by the forces of Syracuse ended Etruscan influence in the western Mediterranean and left Carthage master of this rich trading area.

12 THE RISE OF ROME

The map (below) shows the course of the Tiber, with the Etruscan and Latin cities that grew up around it. Rome was well placed on the trade routes between Etruria and the Greek cities of southern Italy, and on the important salt road which went inland from the coastal salt deposits.

A bronze statue (right) of the famous Etruscan she-wolf, symbol of Rome. According to legend, the wolf suckled Romulus and Remus, founders of the city. To the Etruscans the wolf stood for ferocity. The babies (a later addition in the Renaissance) gave the wolf mother-love significance.

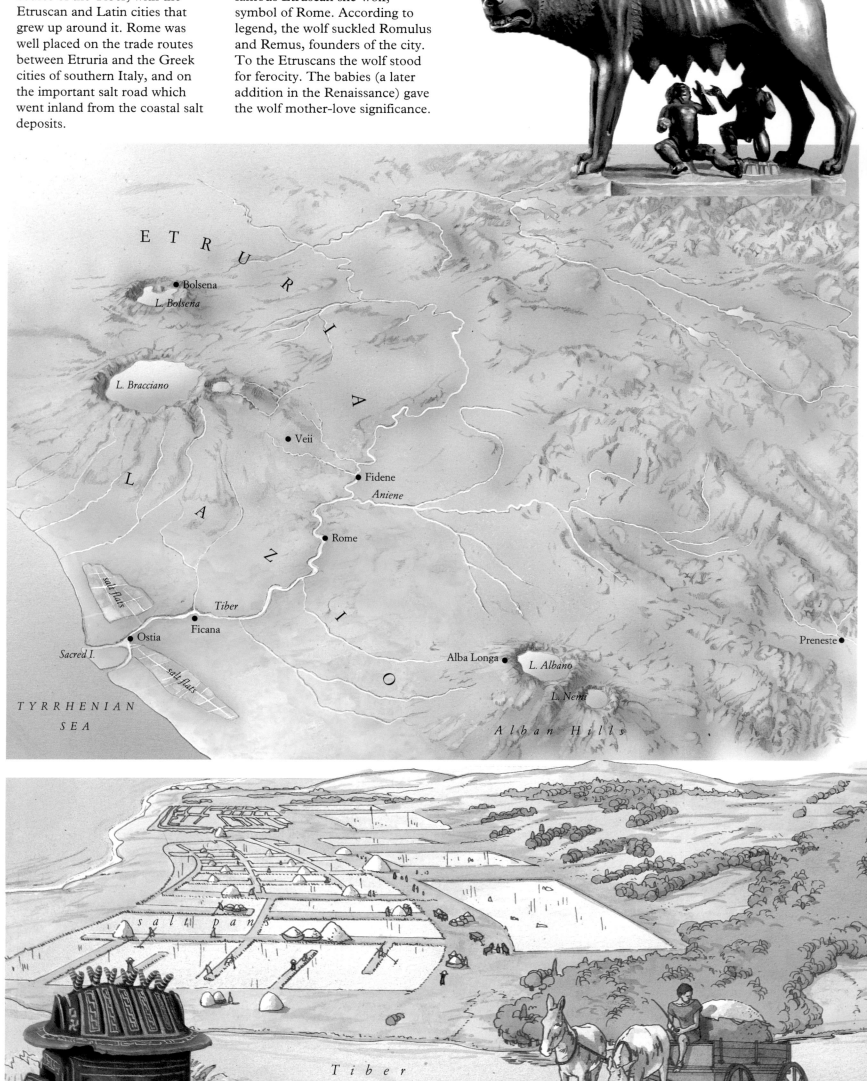

ETRURIA

Bolsena
L. Bolsena

L. Bracciano

Veii

Fidene
Aniene

Rome

LAZIO

salt flats

Tiber

Ostia   Ficana

Sacred I.

salt flats

TYRRHENIAN
SEA

Alba Longa   L. Albano

L. Nemi

Alban Hills

Preneste

salt pans

Tiber

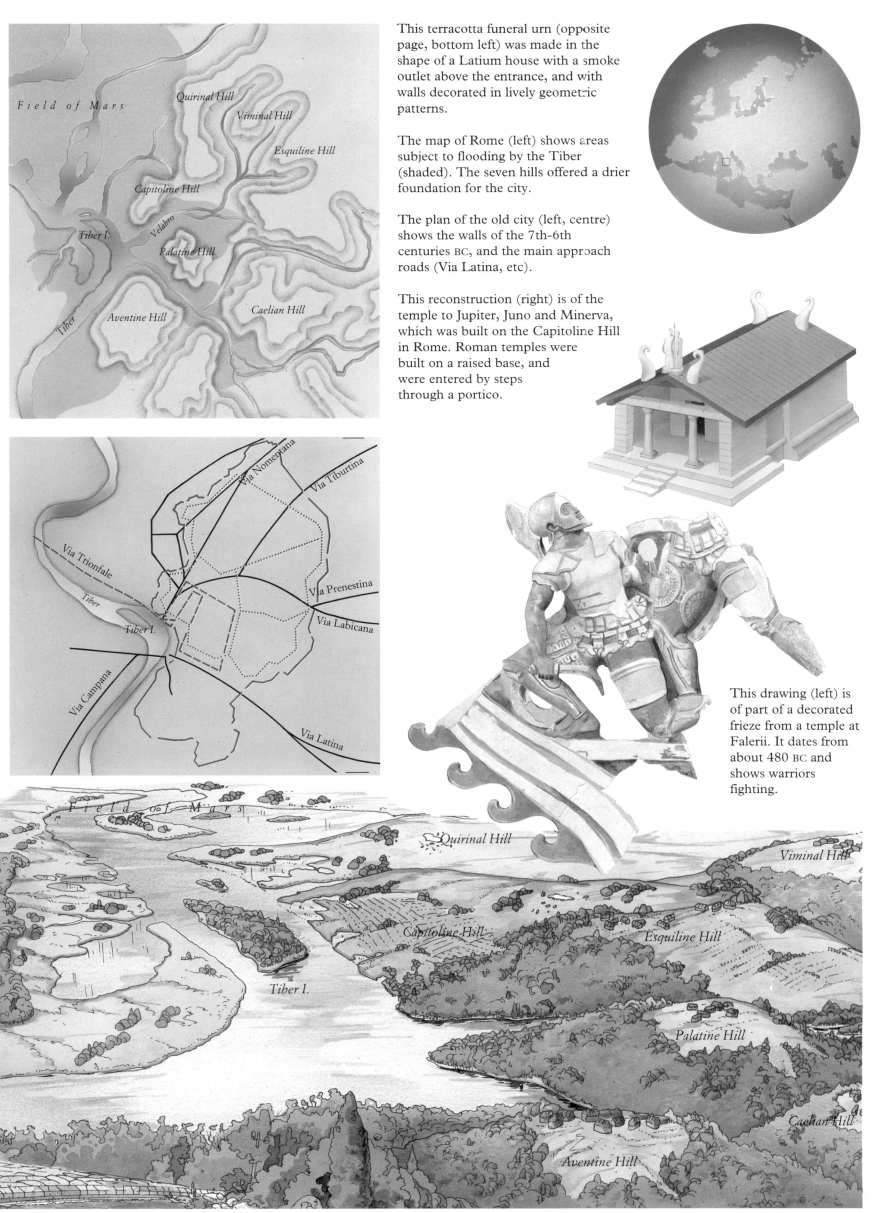

This terracotta funeral urn (opposite page, bottom left) was made in the shape of a Latium house with a smoke outlet above the entrance, and with walls decorated in lively geometric patterns.

The map of Rome (left) shows areas subject to flooding by the Tiber (shaded). The seven hills offered a drier foundation for the city.

The plan of the old city (left, centre) shows the walls of the 7th-6th centuries BC, and the main approach roads (Via Latina, etc).

This reconstruction (right) is of the temple to Jupiter, Juno and Minerva, which was built on the Capitoline Hill in Rome. Roman temples were built on a raised base, and were entered by steps through a portico.

This drawing (left) is of part of a decorated frieze from a temple at Falerii. It dates from about 480 BC and shows warriors fighting.

12 THE RISE OF ROME

A plan of the Forum and Palatine areas of Rome. The Forum area on the Capitoline Hill included places for assembly, shops and markets. The Palatine Hill, where the rich built their homes, is the oldest part of the historic city. The Circus was used for chariot races and other games and spectacles.

Rome was not 'founded' out of nowhere by Romulus and Remus in 753 BC, as tradition and legend tell. Instead, the city grew naturally, like other communities in the Latium region of Italy. The legendary tale came later, when Rome was great.

The first Rome

During the Iron Age, the Italic-speaking peoples of Italy grew in numbers. They built villages along the Tiber river, on the Alban Hills, and along the Tyrrhenian Sea coast away from unhealthy marshes. Later Samnites, Sabines and Oscians mingled with the Latin peoples.

During the 8th century BC, these peoples, who were initially at odds with one another, settled down more peaceably in the first towns of the region. One arose in the Alban Hills, and later became Alba Longa. Another grew on the left (west) bank of the Tiber. This was Rome. The hilly site made a good defensive position, in a loop of the river near the ford or crossing place by Tiber Island. As well as being easily defended, the site controlled important trade routes, including the salt road from the Tyrrhenian coast. This gave Rome contacts with the northern Etruscan cities, and with Greek Italy.

Rome grows and kings rule

The valley between the Palatine and Capitoline Hills became a cattle market and flourishing trade centre for surrounding communities. Housing spread from the Palatine to other sites. The slopes overlooking the Viminal and Esquiline valleys became burial grounds.

Early Rome was governed by a king-priest, who led the cults that were shared by the league of peoples who now

The plan shows the Capitoline Hill, Forum Romanum, Via Sacra, Palatine Hill, Circus Maximus and the Tiber.

lived in the city-state. Tradition, as told by the later historian Livy, has it that Romulus was the first great Roman leader, who led them to war with the Sabines. A Sabine ruler, Numa Pompilius, became king after Romulus – showing that the two peoples, Latins and Sabines, had merged.

Religious rites and processions around the hills of Rome celebrated this union of peoples, and the ceremony continued as a reminder that the city had grown out of co-operation between its peoples. The first four kings of Rome (Romulus, Numa Pompilius, Tullius Ostillius and Ancus Marcius) were alternately Latins and Sabines. The last

The picture (in colour on pages 48/49) shows the view across the River Tiber and the hills of Rome in the days before the walled city. The river was the border between Latium and Etruria, and boats could travel up it a considerable distance. Heavy cargoes were restricted to the lower course, between the River Aniene and the sea.

The cart laden with salt is moving up the road on the Roman side of the river. In the distance are the salt pans, located near to the Tyrrhenian Sea. Salt was a valued commodity, and a source of wealth.

The river is shallow, and can be crossed by a ford near the Tiber Island. This was a key spot on the main Etruscan trade route going south, to Greek cities in southern Italy.

The countryside is fertile, though marshy and subject to flooding. The hills are the safest places for people to build homes. These factors make the site a good one for a city that is destined to become the heart of a mighty empire.

This decorated ostrich egg (right) was found at Vulci, near Rome. The Romans traded with the Etruscans and Greeks, and with peoples around the Mediterranean. Painted eggs like this came from North Africa.

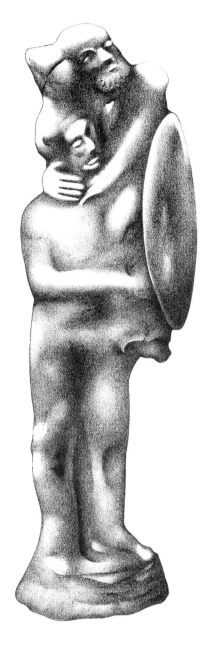

This 5th-century BC terracotta statue (left) comes from Veio. It is of Aeneas carrying his father Anchises. Legend told how Aeneas came to Rome from Troy, with his followers.

three kings were Etruscans: Tarquin the Elder, Servius Tullius and Tarquin the Proud.

Etruscan Rome

It was possible in early Rome for a foreigner to become king, because succession was not hereditary. A foreign king had the advantage of not being seen to take one side against another, in a still-young federation of peoples.

Until the 7th century BC, Etruscan influence on Rome was limited to a supremacy in trade and culture. The Etruscans were not in a position to rule Rome, because of their own divisions. But the presence of Etruscan kings in Rome guaranteed that they kept control of the important trade routes to southern Italy. The Etruscan kings ruled from 616 to 509 BC. They walled the city, and built the temple to Jupiter, Juno and Minerva on the Capitoline Hill. They also gave the Romans their alphabet. Under the Etruscans, Rome became Latium's chief city, covering an area of roughly 1,000 square kilometres (2,500 acres).

A reconstruction of a simple Roman hut (below). It is based on remains found on the Palatine Hill.

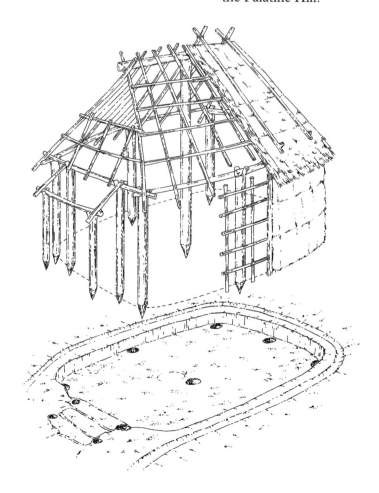

A bronze stopper (right) from a jug or flask in the shape of an animal's head. It dates from the 6th-4th centuries BC.

This dagger (left) is made of bronze and iron. It comes from the Ukraine and dates from the 8th-7th centuries BC.

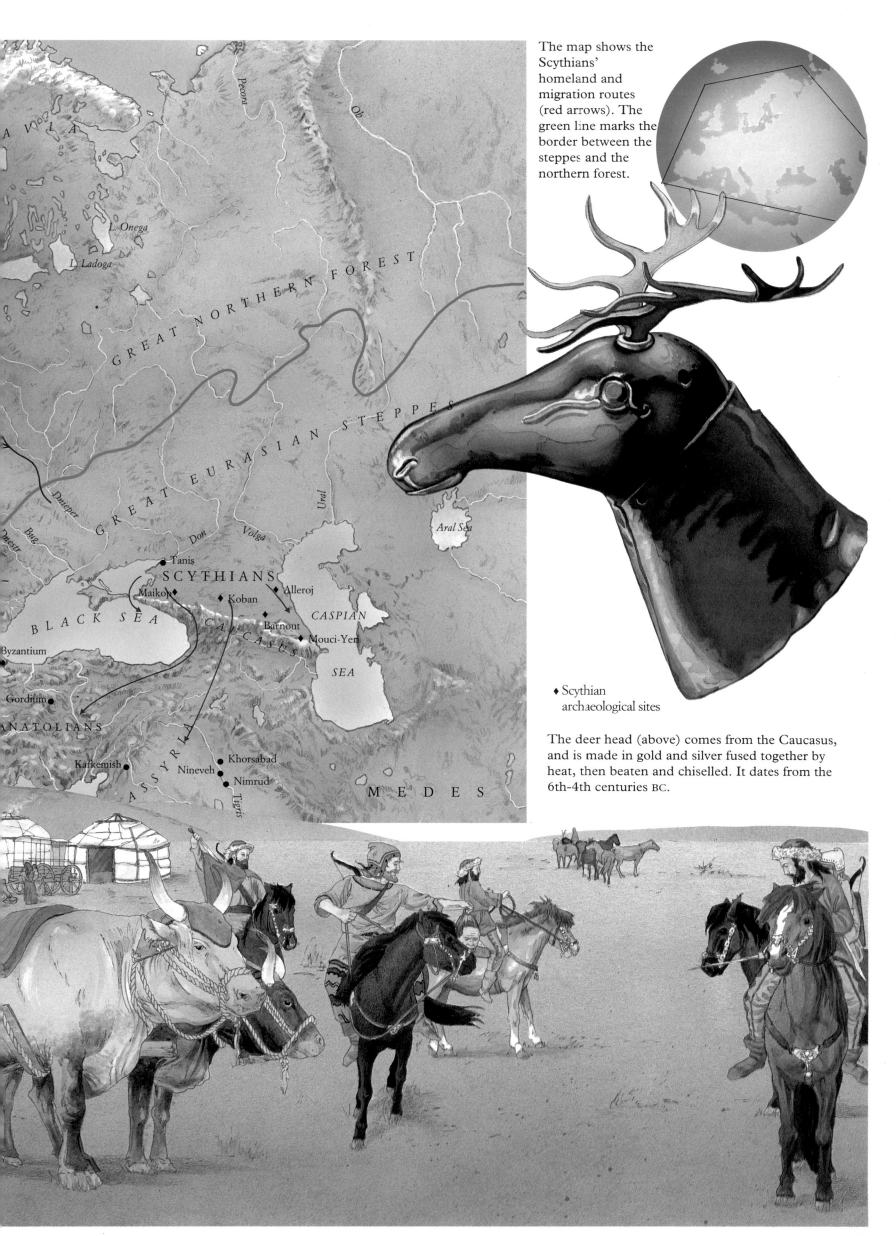

The map shows the Scythians' homeland and migration routes (red arrows). The green line marks the border between the steppes and the northern forest.

♦ Scythian archaeological sites

The deer head (above) comes from the Caucasus, and is made in gold and silver fused together by heat, then beaten and chiselled. It dates from the 6th-4th centuries BC.

13 THE SCYTHIANS

During the 2nd millennium BC, a group of people settled on the steppes (grassy plains) of southern Russia, north of the Black Sea. They shared a method of burying their dead, in wooden-walled tombs. Along with the dead were buried horses and carts. Some of the carts had solid wheels, others were lighter chariots with spoked wheels. These people were the ancestors of the Scythians, a nomadic people who in the 8th century pushed south and west. They became known as the 'distant people'. To the Assyrians they were the Gimmerai, and to the Greeks (who thought them barbarians) the Kymmeroi.

Scythians on the move

The Scythians allied themselves with the Assyrians, and by 611 BC they had reached as far south as Egypt. They moved west into the Carpathian mountains, into Transylvania and Hungary. They made occasional raids into northwest Europe, as far as what are now Belgium and Bavaria. They also traded with these regions, then part of the Hallstatt cultural world (see pages 22/23). Their most thriving trade was across the Black Sea between the region known as Scythia (between the Danube and Don rivers) and the Aegean Sea. They traded furs, slaves and grain in exchange for wine and luxury goods from the more civilized world.

Scythian kings and treasures

The Scythians spoke a language related to the Indo-European Iranian group of languages. Some were farmers, especially those living close to the Black Sea, the Danube basin and the edges of Mesopotamia. Others were wandering herders of cattle, sheep and horses, constantly on the move across the grassy plains of east-central Europe and the

Ukraine. With them they took their heavy carts, their tents and their families.

Men dominated Scythian society. The Scythian chieftain was an all-powerful ruler, served by a class of warrior-nobles who earned their reputation and rank through heroism in battle. Scythians fought on horseback, and excelled as archers with bows and arrows. Their tactics were unique among ancient armies, and Scythian soldiers were feared for their speed and the unpredictability of their attacks. The chieftain commanded loyalty from his warriors. He could have many wives, and his word was law. His funeral was

---

The scene (shown in colour on pages 52/53) depicts Scythians about to leave camp. The heavy cart is pulled by oxen, and from it dangle the heads of two captives. The warriors ride on tough steppe ponies, and are armed with the bows that made Scythians such formidable fighters. The chieftain's horse (left) has an ornate harness. The horse gave the Scythians mobility, but was also a source of meat, along with their cattle.

Scythian women spent their time cooking and looking after children, in the tents of the camp or in the wagons when the group was on the move. The tents in the background are made of poles covered in felt (like the yurts of the Mongols of Asia).

Groups of Scythians travelled in wagon trains across the plains, plundering as they went. When they stayed anywhere, they set up their tents. Warriors rode off to steal sheep and cattle, and to capture slaves. They then moved on, taking their booty with them.

This bronze brooch (opposite page) dates from the 1st millennium BC. The lower part is shaped like an axe. The upper part shows two hunting dogs attacking a stag.

Four horses' heads are skilfully entwined in this ornate piece of tinwork from Slovenia (below).

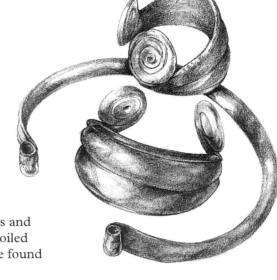

These bronze bracelets and necklaces (right) are coiled and ribbed. They were found in tombs at Koban.

accompanied by the sacrifice of servants and horses.

Kings were buried in rich tombs, stacked with treasures. Human victims were also sacrificed as part of the burial ceremony. Many tombs were looted, but some treasures survive. Scythian goldsmiths were famous for their skill, but craftworkers also made beautiful objects in materials such as felt, skin and wood. Some of these perishable treasures have been preserved in ice tombs in the Altai mountains. Artists created stylized animal figures, including birds, deer and wolves, either complete animals or details such as head and claws. These are connected to the Scythian gods, and endowed with mystical properties so that the everyday world of objects mingled with the magic world of the gods.

This animal (above) is either a horse or a deer. It is made from stamped gold and comes from Hungary.

This decorated axe (right) has geometric patterns incised on it. It comes from the burial site at Koban (800-600 BC).

This bronze pendant (left) is made in the form of a wild sheep, perhaps a mouflon, with curving horns. This is a common Scythian motif. It was also found at Koban.

1400	1300	1200	1100	1000	900	800

| 14th century | 13th century | 12th century | 11th century | 10th century | 9th century |

Greece and the Aegean

Fall of Knossos

Fall of Mycenae

Migrations of northeastern Greeks

First evidence of sculpture: statuettes of warriors, offerings, animals

Destruction of Santorini (Thera)

Fall of Troy

Greek settlements on western coast of Anatolia

Mycenaean culture

Homer
Hesiod

Eastern Europe

Chinese influences in Siberia

Probable Scythian migration from the Caspian to the Ukraine

Scythian art influenced by Chinese art

Central and Western Europe

Lowering of temperature north of the Alps after geological disturbances in the second half of the 13th century BC.

Start of Iron Age

Urnfield people, possible ancestors of the Celts

Possible migration of Bronze Age Atlantic peoples along the great German rivers and mingling with people of the late Unĕtice culture in Bohemia, giving rise to the early Celtic, Illyrian, Italic, and German migrations and the Sea Peoples' expeditions.

Settlement of Ligurian peoples from the Atlantic to northern Italy. Trade with the Greeks. Control of the Rhône estuary, the end of the British tin route.

Northern Europe and the British Isles

Middle of Bronze Age – Imports of blue pottery from Egypt – Arrival of Picts

Rock carvings in Scandinavia show large ocean-going boats similar to Viking longships, four centuries before the Phoenicians

Natural disasters in the second half of the 13th century BC worsen the climate and some prosperous and advanced cultures are wiped out

Invasion of the British Isles by Celts from central Europe

Tomb-builders and Beaker peoples in Ireland

Iberian Peninsula, Italy and Western Mediterranean

Immigration of Italic peoples

Villanovan culture in north-central Italy. Cremation. Nuraghi in Sardinia. Possible arrival of the Etruscans in Italy

Start of Iberian culture in eastern Spain
Iron Age technology introduced

Start of Phoenician colonization

This bronze statue of a Greek hoplite (foot soldier) dates from the Archaic period and comes from Dodona.

North Africa and Egypt

1085 – 900 21st Dynasty. Division of Egypt

950 – 730 22nd Dynasty. The Libyan Shoshenq I reuni

814 Founding of Carthage

Ramses III finally defeats the Sea Peoples

Settlement of Philistines in Palestine

Near East

Iron Age

1160 End of Cassite rule in Babylonia

1020 – 1000 Saul founds the kingdom of Israel

1000 – 966 David King of Israel. Jerusalem capital of Israel

1137 – 1104 Nebuchadrezzar I of Babylon
Renewal of Assyrian power

966 – 926 Solomon reigns during Israel's greatest period

926 Division of Israel into two kingdoms

Israelite Judges' Age in Palestine

Phrygian rule in Anatolia

850 Founding of

1100	1000	900	800

800 | **700** | **600** | **500**

8th century | 7th century | 6th century

Rise of Sparta

776 First Olympiad
750 Start of colonization in the West

660 Tyranny of Cypselus in Corinth

Doric and Ionic styles. Stone temples. First large sculpures.

594 Solon's reforms at Athens
580 Thales of Miletus
566? Reform of Panathenaea
561 Tyranny of Peisistratus
540 Founding of Greek colonies in Asia Minor

Scythians push their neighbours, the Cimmerians, into Asia Minor and move eastwards into the Balkans

Scythian tribes settle in European Russia

Scythian incursions into eastern Germany

Tumulus tombs of Melgunov

Frozen tumuli in the Altai mountains Kurgan tombs in the Ukraine

Treasure of Oxus

Scythian influences on the art of the Medes

Contacts between Altai and Persia (carpets) and Greek art

Contacts between Scythian art and Hallstatt culture

Hallstatt culture

Germanic peoples

Start of La Tène culture

Invasion of the British Isles by German peoples from the Baltic who had adopted the Hallstatt culture

753 Founding of Rome

Start of Greek colonies

Height of Tartessos culture in Spain

Etruscan culture in central Italy. Etruscans resist the expansion of Greek colonies in Italy

654 Founding of Ibiza colony by the Carthaginians. Start of Carthaginian Empire

590 Etruscan infiltration into Latium. Etruscan settlements on the Tiber

578 – 535 Servius Tullius King of Rome

About 540 naval battle in Alalia, Corsica: Etruscans and Carthaginians defeat the Phocian Greeks

534 – 509 Tarquin the Proud, last Etruscan King of Rome

Rome: building of city walls by the Etruscans

Golasecca Iron Age culture in Lombardy. First known Celtic writings

Egypt

750 – 720 23rd Dynasty
750 Founding of Nubian kingdom

720 – 715 24th Dynasty

715 25th Dynasty. Start of Late Period

Revival of Egyptian art; stone and bronze sculptures

525 Cambyses II Great King of Persia conquers Egypt

Age of Prophets in Jewish kingdoms

Sargon II's palace at Khorsabad

725 End of Israel's kingdom

Urartu State

Assyria greatest power in Middle East

Invasion by Cimmerians

Lydian kingdom

Rule of the Achaemenids in Persia

Zoroaster's teachings in Persia

Cambyses I king of the Persians

592 Persian military expedition to Thrace

559 Cyrus II Great King of Persia

Dominance of Medes

547 Cyrus II defeats Croesus, King of Lydia

530 Cambyses II rules Persia

800 | **700** | **600** | **500**

57

15 THE CARTHAGINIANS

By the 6th century BC, Carthage was independent of the Phoenician homeland, and predominant among the states of the western Mediterranean. Its forces protected the Phoenician colonies in the west.

Because its population was too small to man a large army, Carthage recruited mercenaries (hired soldiers) from Libya, Numidia, Mauritania, Sardinia and Iberia. This allowed its own citizens to concentrate on trading and creating enough wealth to pay the soldiers.

As its wealth was based on trade, Carthage was one of the least warlike Mediterranean states. It was reluctant to fight serious wars with its chief rivals, the Greeks of Sicily. The danger of conflict with the Persian king Cambyses, who in 525 conquered Egypt and Cyrenaica, was averted by the attitude of the Phoenicians living under Persian rule who refused to allow their ships to sail against a colony founded by their own kinsmen.

Troubles in Sicily

The first stirrings of trouble in the Mediterranean came from Sicily. There the Greek colonies lagged behind cities on the Greek mainland, which had advanced politically and culturally in the 6th century BC. In many Greek city-states the rule of the landowning nobility was overcome by tyrants, who came to power with the support of disgruntled populations. The tyrants in turn were replaced by regimes that were more or less democratic. However, in Sicily, most city-states were still ruled by nobles or tyrants who felt threatened by new ideas spreading among the merchants and traders.

In Sicily, tyrant rule was unlike that of mainland Greece because it relied on support from the wealthy, not from the

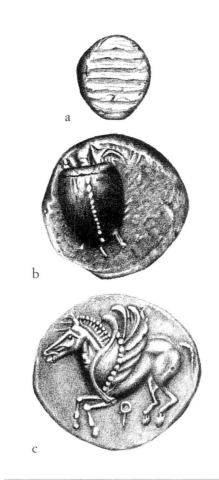

Metal coins like these were made in Lydia in the 7th century BC, and widely used in Greece. They were made of electron, a natural alloy of gold and silver, but later coins were made of pure gold.
a. Ancient coin made of electron, Samos, about 600 BC.
b. Silver double drachma, about 570 BC, minted at Aegina, and stamped with a tortoise mark.
c. A coin from Corinth, about 520 BC, with a winged horse. Corinth was one of the busiest trade links between East and West.

mass of the people. Sicilian rulers, such as Hippocrates of Gela (498 BC) and his successor Gelon, won favour because they guaranteed stability. They also dreamed of greater personal power, and exploited the rivalry with Carthage to create the belief that Greek Sicily had to fight a 'patriotic war' against the Carthaginians. They began to attack Carthaginian colonies in western Sicily. Gelon seized virtually all of Greek Sicily, and in 485 BC moved his capital to Syracuse (which had deposed its own noble rulers). He forced people from subject cities to move there too.

The Carthaginians responded by mounting their own attacks in 480 BC. These coincided (either by design or accident) with the attempt by King Xerxes of Persia to

This picture of a Greek warship, with three banks of oars (a trireme), was discovered on the wall of a house on the island of Delos. Although probably of a later date, the engraving shows a type of ship that was commonly used in the 600s BC by the navies of the Sicilian Greek colonies. The trireme was a symbol of maritime power in the Greek city-states. It was heavier than the fast bireme (with two banks of oars), and so more effective when ramming an enemy ship. It had a single sail, and a large steering oar at the stern.

This map was drawn by the French historian Fernand Braudel. Unusually, it puts the south at the top, as was often done by mapmakers of the Middle Ages. This view emphasizes the size of the African Sahara and the importance of the Mediterranean Sea (known as the Interior Sea in ancient times) as both a divide and a bridge between Africa, Asia and Europe. The sea was a vital crossroads for cultures. With its populated islands and peninsulas giving easy access to inland regions, the Mediterranean was relatively easy to navigate. Around its shores grew up ports and cities, linked by shipping routes and roads. It was a region of the world that offered an unusual combination of conditions conducive to the spread of goods, cultures, art and ideas.

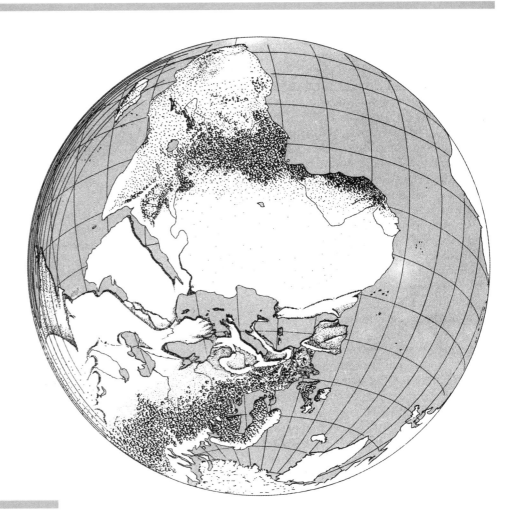

conquer Greece, and it served to unite the Greeks of Sicily. The tyrants of Agrigento, Gela and Syracuse formed an alliance to withstand the threat.

These skirmishes indicate how the western Mediterranean in this period was affected both by Greek colonization, expanding westward, and by economic considerations (trade and the need to protect trade routes and trade settlements).

New ideas and ways of seeing the world

The changing world was introducing new philosophies – in which knowledge was seen not as supernatural revelation but as a logical search for the truth. The work of philosopher-scientists such as Anaxagoras (500?-428 BC), Thales (640-546 BC), Anaximander (611-547 BC) and Hecataeus (6th-5th century BC) explored the natural world, seeking to explain it. Others such as Pythagoras (500s BC), Parmenides and Heraclitus (6th-5th century) were equally concerned with the relationship between nature and the divine, the order of the world and the soul of man. All these great scholars were rationalists, relying on mind more than mysticism. A new age was dawning.

Thales

Anaximander

Hecataeus

The Greek port of Miletus in Asia Minor was a centre for scholars and geographers. The earliest scholar we know of was Thales. He pictured the world as a sphere, the lower half of which was filled with water. The earth was a disc floating on the water. The upper half was full of air, and above it were the heavenly bodies (stars and planets). Anaximander was Thales' pupil. He imagined the earth to be a disc surrounded by mountains, which enclosed the waters of the oceans. Hecataeus of Miletus, who was both a diplomat and a geographer, drew this map of the Greek world (the Mediterranean) on a copper disc. Italy, Greece and the Nile river are clearly shown. He wrote a travel book called 'A Tour Round the World' which was widely used by other scholars.

GLOSSARY

The Twelve Labours of Hercules, illustrated with drawings based on frescoes, sculptures and wall-paintings of Archaic and Classical Greece. The myth of Herakles (Hercules) son of the god Zeus and the mortal Alcmene, who in turn was made a god, was common to many Mediterranean cultures. His famous tasks, his purification and ascension to Mount Olympus were metaphors for the human struggle, and the victory of life over death.

FIRST LABOUR Hercules kills the Nemean lion and wears its skin.

SECOND LABOUR Hercules slays the Hydra of Lerna, a monster with nine heads.

THIRD LABOUR Hercules captures the Arcadian stag.

FOURTH LABOUR Hercules hunts the Erymanthian boar.

FIFTH LABOUR Hercules drives away the birds of Lake Stymphalus.

Aboriginal Describes the original inhabitants of a place.

Amber Transparent fossilized resin that was an important trade item, valued for making necklaces.

Archaeologist Person who studies prehistory and ancient history, often excavating sites to do so.

Archaic An early period in a civilization or in art.

Archer Soldier armed with a bow and arrow.

Aristocracy Government by the best or outstanding citizens; ruling class.

Augurer Person who foretells the future, by observing the behaviour of live animals and inspecting the entrails of dead ones.

Autonomy The right of self-government.

Basalt Rock formed from volcanic lava.

Beaker culture Neolithic culture named after the typical shape of its pottery – like an upturned bell.

Bureaucracy Government by a central administration, or the civil servants or officials who run a country.

Celts People who originated in central Europe and spread as far west as Britain. They were one of the first European peoples to make iron tools.

Chalcolithic The period between the Neolithic (New Stone Age) and the Bronze Age, when copper was first used.

Chariot Two-wheeled vehicle pulled by one or more horses, and used to carry warriors into battle.

Civil war Armed struggle between citizens of the same state for political or social reasons.

Clan Tribe or family group that stands together.

Coalition League or alliance of states and peoples with a common military or political goal.

Colony Settlement founded by a people in a territory not its own.

Commerce Trade.

Confederation Union of neighbour states with common interests.

Cosmos The universe as a whole. A cosmogony is a theory of the origin of the universe.

Cremation Disposal of a corpse by burning.

Cult System of religious worship, with its own rules and ceremonies, often practised in secret.

Cyclopean Describes fortress walls made of gigantic stones fitted together, as at Mycenae.

Deity A god or goddess.

Democracy Government elected by all the people of a state.

Elite Social class or group with the privileges of rank; a ruling nobility.

Epic Narrative story or poem celebrating the deeds of one or more legendary heroes, who may personify the national character.

Excavation Process by which archaeologists uncover layers of long-buried ruins, revealing buildings, tombs and other remains below the surface.

Exile Absence, sometimes imposed as a punishment, of a person from his or her homeland for a long period.

Felt Kind of cloth made without weaving, using natural fibres (wool, horse- and ox-hair) which mat together.

Fertile Describes land that is good for growing crops, or animals that have many offspring.

Funerary To do with funerals.

Galley Ship with one large sail and banks of oars.

Grave goods Articles, such as furniture, clothes and jewellery, placed in a tomb for a dead person to use in the next world.

Indo-Europeans Farming and herding peoples originating in Eurasia. They spoke related languages and shared some customs.

Kurgan culture Semi-nomadic culture from Russia that spread west across Europe. 'Kurgan' means burial mound.

League A union of peoples, or states, for mutual advantage.

Limestone Type of sedimentary rock used for building. Marble is a form of limestone that has been hardened by heat and pressure underground.

SIXTH LABOUR
Hercules cleans the stables of King Augeas.

SEVENTH LABOUR
Hercules steals the horse of King Diomedes.

EIGHTH LABOUR
Hercules captures the bull of Minos.

NINTH LABOUR
Hercules obtains the girdle of Hippolyta, Queen of the Amazons.

TENTH LABOUR
Hercules brings back the cattle of the monster Geryon.

ELEVENTH LABOUR
Hercules steals the golden apples from the Tree of Life in the Hesperides.

TWELFTH LABOUR
Hercules descends to the Underworld and captures the three-headed watchdog Cerberus.

Linear B Form of writing, used by the Mycenaeans but of Minoan origin.

Lost wax process Method of casting figures and models, in which wax is used to surround a model and line a pottery mould in its exact shape. Bronze poured into the mould can harden and be removed later by melting the wax.

Megalithic Describes huge stone slabs used as monuments during the Stone and Copper Ages.

Migration Movement of peoples (or animals) from one region to another for settlement. Emigrants move out, immigrants move in.

Minoan Describes the civilization and culture of Crete in the 2nd millennium BC, named after the mythical King Minos.

Monopoly System in which certain goods can be sold or produced by one person or group only.

Mycenaean Describes the culture and civilization of Mycenae, in Greece, and the surrounding region in the 2nd millennium BC.

Neolithic The New Stone Age, a period characterized by farming, working with polished stone tools, and the invention of pottery.

Nomads People with no permanent homes who wander in search of grazing for their sheep, goats, horses or other animals.

Nordic Northern European, especially Scandinavian.

Nuraghi Cone-shaped stone towers, built for defence by people of Pre-Roman Sardinia.

Obsidian Hard, glassy, black volcanic rock.

Olympus Highest mountain in Greece, believed by the ancient Greeks to be the home of the gods, who were known as the Olympian gods.

Oracle Medium of divine revelation; a place or person through whom (it was believed) a god or gods responded to people's questions.

Panhellenic Of all Greece. Hellene is another name for a Greek.

Pantheon Collective name for all the Greek or Roman gods or a temple dedicated to them. Pantheism is the worship of many gods.

Peninsula Strip or larger area of land jutting out into the sea. Spain and Portugal, for example, share the large Iberian Peninsula.

Polis Greek city-state.

Punic Carthaginian.

Seal Engraved stone or metal cylinder used to stamp an image or decorative motif on soft clay or wax.

Secular Belonging to a lay, or non-religious, society.

Shaft tomb Tomb of a ruler or important person, made by digging a tunnel into the ground, as at Mycenae.

Site Place where research and archaeological studies are carried out into the remains of buildings, tombs, roads and other features.

Steppes Treeless grassy plains of east-central Europe and Asia, inhabited in ancient times by wandering nomads.

Stylize To represent something, such as a person or animal, by simplifying its features and reducing them to essential details in a picture.

Terracotta Kind of brownish-red pottery made from baked clay and sand.

Torc or **torque** Necklace in the form of a twisted metal band.

Tribal Describes a tribe or group of related families, usually under a chief.

Tumulus Mound of earth and stones raised above the tomb of a dead person.

Urban Describes the city or city life.

Urn Container holding the ashes of a cremated person.

Urnfield culture Bronze Age culture that penetrated central Europe from the east, characterized by the custom of cremating bodies and sealing the ashes in urns.

Votive Describes an object offered in fulfilment of a vow in religious worship.

Zeus King of the gods on Mount Olympus and chief of the gods of ancient Greece. To the Romans, Zeus was Jupiter.

INDEX